ORDINARY PEOPLE EXTRAORDINARY GOD

17 PERSONAL STORIES OF LIVES TRANSFORMED BY THE LOVE OF GOD

"I have known Rick Schatz for twenty years and have collaborated with him in many ministry situations. He is a selfless servant of Jesus, the real deal. I also know many of the people whose stories Rick has compiled, and he has captured these amazing people beautifully. You will be encouraged by these stories and see that in Jesus you can bloom right where you are planted. We are all bit players in the story of our supreme King, and this book, *Ordinary People Extraordinary God*, reminds us that our significance is not in our achievements but rather in what Jesus has done!"

> —DENIS BEAUSEJOUR, Pastor,
> Mariemont Community Church

"Within these pages, Rick Schatz introduces you to ordinary believers who have become extraordinary servers. Their stories are engaging, inspiring, and instructive. As you read, you will discover a common decision they share as followers of Jesus—and it changed everything. Spoiler alert! Reading this will mark the beginning of your release for remarkable Kingdom service!"

> —IZRAEL GAITHER, Retired National Commander,
> Salvation Army

"We are blessed and encouraged when we read how God uses ordinary people in His Word—Moses, Abraham, Joshua, the disciples. All of them contributed to the Father's plan for His people. Rick humbly presents ordinary people of our day. They continue to fulfill God's plan for restoration and transformation. As they serve the Lord, may we see their good works and glorify our Father in heaven."

—SHARRON HUDSON, Commissioner, Salvation Army, USA National Headquarters

"What an encouraging work, chronicling the lives of people serving our awesome God. The key theme of *Ordinary People Extraordinary God* is hopeful and inspiring, a great reminder of God's bigger plan for our lives, His church, and our world. You will be encouraged by these stories of transformation and the amazing grace, love, and power of our Lord."

—JASPER HALL, President, pureHope

"*Ordinary People Extraordinary God* bears cogent witness to the fact that there is no such thing as an 'ordinary Christian.' With its colorful variety of narratives that illustrate God using Christians like you and me to do extraordinary things, this book is a recipe for encouragement to the believer who desires a life of usefulness to the Lord Jesus Christ."

—CHRISTOPHER JERO, PhD, Mars Hill Academy

"Through the ages, the church has been nourished by stories of the saints. Rick Schatz has accomplished a great service in delivering to us portraits of contemporary everyday Christians whose lives witness the power of the gospel. We would do well to imitate them as they imitate our Lord."

— DR. STEVEN LANGDON, Family Medicine,
Lawrenceburg, Indiana

"Have you ever felt like God only used the famous and popular people of this world to do great things? And yet, all through history, God has done just the opposite. God has used people who are weak, unpopular, and reluctant to do great things to change the world. In this book, *Ordinary People Extraordinary God*, you will encounter regular people whom God has used to do amazing things because they simply wanted to serve the Lord. I have been blessed to have known Rick Schatz for many years and have watched him in his relentless desire to serve the Lord. In these pages that he has before you, you will encounter regular people who offered their lives to be used by God. You too can be one of those people!"

— REV. DR. JOHN LEWIS, Presbyterian Church,
Hamilton, Ohio

"'Empowerment.' I hear this word often, but I see it rarely. While many of us believe that the power of the Holy Spirit indwells Christians, and that God has used 'ordinary people for extraordinary contributions,' we nonetheless struggle to believe that the ordinary person God might choose to use is us! In this wonderful book, *Ordinary People Extraordinary God*, Rick Schatz showcases ordinary people, just like you and me, who have simply had the faith to step forward and then supernaturally stepped out in mighty service for God. I encourage you to read this book, both for inspiration *and* instruction to bring extraordinary Kingdom work to life through you."

—CHUCK PROUDFIT, President, At Work on Purpose

"This book will inspire you! Rick Schatz has been a dear friend and colleague for decades, and he has written a book that will help you find fresh meaning in your life. If you're wondering whether God can use you, the answer is a resounding yes! Rick offers real-life examples of 'ordinary' people, many of whom I know, whom God has used in truly meaningful ways. Let this message sink into your soul. It just may shape you in profound ways."

—PAUL J. MAURER, PhD, President, Montreat College

"Over the last forty years that I have known Rick Schatz, he has always had a primary focus on sharing Jesus Christ with a broken, hurting world. I also know many of the people Rick writes about in this book. Each of them has demonstrated over time their commitment to the Lord by being obedient to God's call on their lives. These humble servants have impacted countless thousands of men, women, and children with the gospel. Read *Ordinary People Extraordinary God*! You will be inspired, and perhaps you too will answer God's call."

— BRAD MUELLER, Executive Director,
Jobs Plus Employment Network, and
Vice President, City Gospel Mission

"One of the great joys of being a part of the family of God is to know a person such as Rick Schatz, who has been used by the Lord in wonderful ways. He has captured the stories of ordinary people whom our extraordinary God uses, simply by people making themselves available, thus leaving a legacy for time and eternity."

— DR. TOM TRASK, Retired General Superintendent,
Assemblies of God

"In an era when our culture's fixation on 'celebrity' has too often seeped into the church, Rick Schatz's stories of men and women simply (and quietly) obeying God's call that results in historic Kingdom building work is a wonderful corrective and reminder. What is extraordinary about service for Jesus Christ is not the person, it's the God we serve. When the supernatural power of the Holy Spirit 'shows up' in the life of any believer committed to His call in their life, there's no limit to what God can do. Expect to be encouraged, blessed, and challenged by these ordinary men and women used in extraordinary ways by an infinite God whose 'eyes range throughout the earth to strengthen those whose hearts are fully committed to Him.'"

— JEFF JEREMIAH, Stated Clerk,
Evangelical Presbyterian Church

"I have known and worked with Rick Schatz for several years as a donor and ultimately as a board member of the Prayer Covenant. Rick earned my respect instantly as I related to him as a businessman turned ministry leader. Rick is always prepared, consistently accurate in business and Kingdom matters, visibly passionate, and truly excited about Kingdom work. Regardless of the setting, Rick energizes every room he enters. I look forward to seeing all that God intends to accomplish through *Ordinary People Extraordinary God.*"

— WILLIAM TRICK, Developer, Outback,
and Board Member, Prayer Covenant

ORDINARY PEOPLE EXTRAORDINARY GOD

17 PERSONAL STORIES OF LIVES TRANSFORMED BY THE LOVE OF GOD

RICK SCHATZ
WITH STEPHEN EYRE

HIGH BRIDGE BOOKS
HOUSTON

Contents

Dedication

This book is dedicated to the ordinary Christians of the world, who are called to do great things for God. The problem is that many of us are sitting in the pews believing that only the pastors, priests, or "great" people are to do work for the King. But it is clear that God calls every believer to participate in His work and that He equips us for His ministry of service to a broken and hurting world. He gives strength, power, and gifts for the work. He gives the opportunity for each of us to have lives of fulfillment and joy in and from Him.

My hope and prayer is that you will be inspired and encouraged as you read the stories of what others have done for the glory of Christ. You can do it. God says so. All for His glory!

Introduction

News outlets around the world reported the passing of Reverend Billy Graham on February 21, 2018. Reverend Graham was known as a great evangelist who had preached the gospel of Jesus around the world for fifty years. He had preached to live audiences of over 210 million people in 185 countries. In his crusades, Graham insisted that churches from many denominations be included, crossing racial and ethnic lines. He was known as America's preacher and the pastor to Presidents.

Dr. R. C. Sproul was born in 1938 and went to be with the Lord on December 14, 2017, at the age of seventy-eight. Sproul received a master of divinity from Pittsburgh-Xenia Theological Seminary and had two doctoral degrees as well. In 1971, he started Ligonier Ministries and began his life work of teaching philosophy, theology, and the Bible. Through the monthly magazine known as *Tabletalk*, Sproul has reached millions with the truth of God's inerrant Word. He was the author of more than one hundred books and was admired and appreciated by many.

C. S. Lewis has been called by many the Christian community's strongest apologist of the twentieth century. His books have been read by millions around the world, including both children and adults. His amazing imagination has stirred his readers to consider the truth of Jesus and the gospel. His book, *The Lion, the Witch and the Wardrobe*, has sold more than eighty-five million copies,

ranking it among the one hundred highest selling published books in history. His works have been carried on
through movies and television productions since his death
in 1963.

Despite persecution, the growth of God's church continues in amazing ways in places such as Africa, the Middle East, and India. Through just one evangelistic
ministry, India Gospel League, more than twenty-five
thousand house churches have been planted in the last
thirty years. Ministries such as Wycliffe Bible Translators
are reaching unreached people groups, putting the Word
of God in their native languages. Completion of the Great
Commission, the good news to every tribe and tongue, is
within reach for the first time in history.

These and other stories of many other Christians and
ministries thrill the hearts and minds of God's people.
These individuals and ministries are doing great things for
God. They are being used by God through the power of
the Holy Spirit to bring God's Kingdom to earth.

But the question before us is how do we as "ordinary
Christians" respond to such reports? On the one hand, we
are thrilled and excited to see what God is doing through
these gifted and capable leaders. But the question asked
by many is, "What can I do?". I am just an ordinary person
who loves Jesus, but I don't have any great skills. I am not
famous, nor will I ever be. I have no seminary degrees or
PhDs. I do not have the imagination or creative genius of a
writer such as C. S. Lewis. What am I called to do to make
an impact for the Kingdom?

The Biblical Narrative of God Using Ordinary People for His Glory

As we consider these important questions, let us look at three biblical examples to see whether we can glean any insight into how God works through His ordinary people. Let's start with David. He became Israel's greatest king, but he started small. He was the youngest and the least in his family, assigned to shepherd the family's herd of sheep. His older brothers were the stars. But God chose David, the least and the youngest, to be king of His people. David united all twelve tribes of Israel into one strong nation. God gave victory over the enemies of Israel through this anointed leader.

Next, let's consider Gideon the judge. He was called by God to defeat the Midianites, one of Israel's constantly harassing enemies. God called, but Gideon was reluctant to answer the call. He didn't even look like a good candidate. He was a member of the least of the tribes of Israel. He was fearful, maybe even a bit cowardly. In fact, he made every effort to avoid the call. He even insisted that God answer two fleeces to prove that the call was real. When he did answer and went into battle, God sent over 90 percent of his army back home so that the victory would clearly belong to God and His power, not to Gideon.

The last biblical character I want to consider is Moses. The people of Israel had been enslaved in Egypt for four hundred years. God heard the cries of His people and called Moses to lead them to freedom. But Moses, like Gideon, did not want to answer God's call. He objected to being God's prophet due to his lack of eloquence, so God provided him with his brother, Aaron, as a partner. Moses ultimately was used by God to lead over two million Israelites out of slavery and bondage into the Promised Land.

The Biblical Calling and the Need

In 1 Corinthians 1:26–29, God makes His calling on each of our lives absolutely clear. The passage teaches us that God calls those who are not wise by human standards. He calls those who are not rich, influential, or famous. He calls the ordinary, the lowly by worldly standards, to accomplish His will on earth. He calls the weak of this world to do extraordinary things in building His Kingdom. The great news is that when God calls, He equips and provides the gifts and skills needed to do His work through the power and presence of His Holy Spirit. In using ordinary people as His servants and workers, He gets all the glory.

Mission and ministry are there before us. Jesus says in Matthew 9:37–38 that the field is ripe unto harvest, but the workers are few. The opportunity for serving God is before each of us. He is calling each of us, and the need is great.

What About You and Me?

Even though David, Moses, and Gideon started small, they ended up being names we all know. Sermons are preached about them! You and I, most likely, will never be "names".

Don't worry about it! Relax in God's call on your life. You may have never heard of many of God's choice servants that are found in the Bible. What about Bezalel,

Tychicus, Tertius, and Silvanus? They are mentioned in the narratives of Scripture, but we don't hear sermons about them. Bezalel was one of the craftsmen who constructed the tabernacle for Israel. Tychicus, Tertius, and Silvanus were scribes who wrote the letters Paul dictated to the first churches. What about Epaenetus, Andronicus, or Junias? They receive a mention from Paul in the greetings to the first Christians in Rome, but we don't know much of any significance about them.

So, when we think about some of the great Christian leaders of history and then consider how God has used them, we must rethink what God is calling us to do. God does not need our greatness, skills, or brilliance. He simply needs our willingness and availability. God has and will use ordinary people like you and me to fulfill the Great Commandment and the Great Commission. He will change His world for His glory through each of His people who will answer His call on their lives.

But I Can't Do Anything

But even in the light of the biblical models and God's clear calling of ordinary people to do His work we are tempted to say, "I am a nobody and can't do much for God." There are many reasons that so many of us struggle with a sense of significance. Perhaps we struggle because of our family experience, our social standing when we were in high school, or some other reason. Whatever it is, many of us deep inside fear we are not good enough or smart enough or capable enough to do anything important for God. But we must not listen to these messages—either from ourselves or from others. Instead we must listen to God, and

He says we are more than enough. He says He can and does use ordinary Christians to do His work and to accomplish great things for Him. In fact, I believe God is saying that there are no ordinary Christians at all!

Listen to God's messages for and to us. Philippians 4:13 teaches, "I can do all this through him who gives me strength." Do we really hear that? Colossians 1:27 says that Christ dwells in every believer and that He is our hope of glory. Ephesians 3:20 teaches that the power that the Father used in raising His only Son from the grave is the power that is at work in every Christian. Yes, when God calls, He equips and empowers. He gives His gifts to His people. You may have the gift of preaching or teaching, but most of the time we are given gifts such as faith, or service, or helps. But in every case God gives the gifts to His people for His service and His glory.

One of the most amazing truths of the entire Bible is what Jesus says to His disciples in John 14:12, when He teaches that His disciples will not only do what He has been doing but even greater things than He has done. This is hard to imagine, but it comes from the words of Jesus Himself. Think about it. Christians have now spread the gospel to every country in the world. There are now more than two billion followers of Jesus. Christians you have never heard of have spread the gospel, built schools and hospitals, and serve the "least of these." All of this is done for the glory of our God and King.

The Bottom Line

When ordinary Christians listen to the message of God about who we are and what we can do for God, we live out the promise of Jesus that He has come to give life in its fullness. This is the promise of Jesus for each of His followers found in John 10:10. This is life that is thrilling, exciting, fulfilling, and challenging all at the same time.

This message from God about who we are is the theme of a contemporary Christian song titled "You Say" by Lauren Daigle. In the song, Daigle contrasts the messages of the world that we all hear with the message of God. She concludes that she will believe God and not the negative messages of the world, and she is right in doing so! She celebrates God's message for her, and we should do the same.

1

From Brokenness to Service

Jean Ellison

I have known Jean Ellison for more than thirty years, *but it has primarily been through her son, Mike. Mike and I were members at the College Hill Presbyterian Church for many years. Then, in 2013, Mike asked me to serve on the board of advisers for his company, the Ellison Group. During this time my relationship with Jean became closer, and then it really changed in the summer of 2018, when Mike died suddenly of a heart attack. Since Mike's death, my time with Jean has been focused on prayer, sharing tears, and celebrating Mike's life.*

Jean Ellison had to be included in this book because her story starts as one of great family brokenness without Christ but ends with great faith and a powerful life in and for Jesus. She comes from a family of seventeen children and was raised in extreme poverty. Family relationships, simply put, were broken and terrible. Jean not only survived after leaving home at the age of fourteen, but she has come to a wonderful, life-changing relationship with the living God. She loves Jesus. As she grew in her love for her Lord, she determined to serve others with love and compassion. Her ministry has been as a hospice nurse professionally and in showing the love of Jesus to hundreds of patients and their families. She has modeled the caring, gentle spirit of her Savior.

So Jean, in the minds of many, would not have been destined for any impact on the world, but those who don't believe in the power of God to change things have been proven wrong. Jean has blessed countless others and continues even after her retirement to minister to many the grace and love of Jesus. Her story is an amazing one. She is someone that the world would discount but who has done great and wonderful things for the King of Kings.

Her confidence in God is shown clearly in her response to the death of her son, Mike. Through the tears she has come to the place where she has said to God, "I give you thanks for letting me raise my son for sixty-three years. Now you have received him back into your loving arms. I praise you for the gift you gave me." Very few people who have come from such brokenness in their families have come to know our Lord and then have served others as Jesus taught us in Matthew 25. Jean has served the sick and dying in ways that challenge and inspire all followers of Jesus.

Jean's Story

I was born June 28, 1936, in Manchester, Kentucky, into a family of seventeen children. I was right in the middle of eleven girls and six boys. My family was broken and poor. My father was an alcoholic and moonshiner. We lived in a three-room house with no inside facilities. In the midst of all of that, I would describe my childhood as impoverished. My father didn't believe in education, and by the time I was eight years old, I was ordered to stay home and cook for the family.

The little schooling I had was in a two-room schoolhouse five miles away. I loved going to school. The conflict between my father's demands and the school kept me from any significant experience of learning. I faced problems such as having no shoes to wear when I entered the ninth grade. Upon returning from school one day at the age of fourteen, my father, as he had done many times before, began to beat me. I screamed at him and said if he didn't stop that I would leave home and he would never see me again. The beating continued, and as I threatened, I did leave. I went to live with my older brother in Cincinnati.

My primary role in Cincinnati was taking care of my brother's two children, at that time, three and five years old. Even though my life was better than it had been, I was seeking a way out. I lied about my age and began work when I was fourteen. I moved to a dormitory facility run by the Methodist church. Bob Ellison, who was to become my husband, drove by this church on his way home one day. He was older than I was and in the Navy. He was soon shipped off overseas. I didn't really think about him much.

The Journey to Jesus

While he was away, a friend of mine in the boardinghouse, Jewell Taylor, invited me to go to a movie about Billy Graham. I went, heard the message of the gospel, and committed my life to Jesus. The impact on my life was both immediate and significant. My mouth, which had previously been filled with filthy language, was cleaned up. For the first time I could remember, I had real joy and peace. I developed a great hunger for church and the Word of God. I went to church Sunday morning, Sunday evening, and Wednesday evening.

When Bob returned to Cincinnati, he called me up and invited me to church and then to go out drinking. That was a conflict! I was confused but still interested. He continued to pursue me, and we developed a very positive relationship. We were married in 1954.

My first son, Mike, was born in 1955. I gave him to the Lord and prayed for his salvation and asked that he grow to be a servant of Christ. As a teenager, Mike committed his life to Jesus, which was an answer to my many prayers. During this time in which Mike committed his life to Jesus, my husband, Bob, did so as well. The special blessing of our marriage was that Bob's father became my father. We had a wonderful relationship.

Despite the broken relationship I had with my natural father, the Lord called me to show him grace and love and to forgive him for the ways he had treated me. I began to write letters to him regularly, feeling a great burden for his soul. Initially he told me he wasn't interested. However, after fourteen years of prayers and letters, my dad came to faith.

My Calling to Serve

I knew that God was calling me to serve Him, but I didn't know how. Did He want me to be a missionary or a nurse? It wasn't clear. I began to study as a beautician. As my kids grew, I felt I should quit to spend time at home.

When they got into college, I began attending the women's Bible studies at College Hill Presbyterian Church. I experienced great spiritual growth. At that time, I was learning from every Christian I met.

I attended a seminar at College Hill on death and dying. This was an introduction to the ministry of hospice. I clearly heard God's calling—I was to be a hospice nurse. I knew I needed a GED to begin nursing school and got it. I was working part time at Christ's Hospital. My daughter, Patty, was in nursing school at the University of Cincinnati when I also began my studies there. I found that ironic and amusing. It was a good experience but challenging. When I started, there were twelve students in their thirties and forties. At the end of the courses, I was the only one left. I received great encouragement from the women at the nursing school who helped me with basic subjects such as English, math, and sociology. I felt God's great caring support.

My studies were not without challenges. One of my teachers told me that I would never make it and she would never pass me. I told her I felt the calling of God, "I need this class." Several of my peers went to the administration and complained on my behalf. Their intercession for me helped, but it wasn't enough. I moved my studies to Bethesda Hospital and graduated from there in 1982, at the age of forty-six.

I applied for a nursing position at Deaconess Hospital and was initially turned down as there were no openings. However, eventually I was offered a position on the third shift, and I took it. I continually asked for God's help, and He always made a way. Eventually I was blessed to be voted the best nurse of the year. The husband of one of my patients nominated me for the Cincinnati Woman of the Year award!

I served as a regular hospice nurse for twelve years and eventually became the manager of that nursing group. I was told I wasn't qualified because I didn't have a master's in nursing. That was amusing, as I didn't have a bachelor's' degree. I got the position anyway!

One nursing experience stands out. A thirty-two-year-old woman who was in hospice care had a staph infection. Everyone, including her, thought she was going to die. I went to God in prayer and asked others to join me. God answered those prayers, and the woman was completely healed. This was God's great gift to her and to me. I learned what it was like to be close to death and call out for help. This helped me care for others with greater compassion.

I retired as a hospice nurse in April 1999. Since that time, I have been given the gift of spending lots of time in Scripture. The Gospel of John was become especially important to me. I have read through the entire Scriptures every year since my retirement.

My son, Mike, passed away suddenly of a heart attack in 2018. He died in my living room. Despite this great loss, I have come to the place where I give thanks to God that He gave me my son for sixty-three years. I am so glad he lived his life as a devoted follower of Jesus. Being thankful has been hard, but I am learning.

Author's Note

In completing Jean's story, I thought it would be useful to share the perspective of her grandson Andy.

Andy writes:

When I think about my grandmother, three things are most important to me: her devotion to reading the Bible, her sharing the gospel with others, and the incredible spiritual conversations that we have had over the years.

Grandma has had a disciplined practice of starting everyday by reading the Scriptures. Her goal has been to read through the entire Bible each year, and she has done so for the last twenty years. Her Bible is littered with her notes about particular verses that have touched her life. She often puts dates by these notes, and it is so challenging to me to see her practice of reading through God's Word year after year.

Despite the fact that Grandma is small in stature, she has the courage of a lion in sharing the gospel with those around her. Whether it is the cable TV man, a worker at a neighborhood store, or someone she passes on the street, she is always ready to ask about Jesus. She shares with warmth, grace, and a genuine love for those who don't know her Savior. She is so engaging with easy conversations, and I am confident that many will be in heaven because of the "seeding and watering" that Grandma has done.

Maybe the best of Grandma's life with me has been the many, many spiritual conversations we have had. She always takes the time to talk. She is never too busy to share her thoughts about Jesus, the Bible, and living for her Lord. Just like her sharing the gospel with others, these conversations were easy. They are part of her life, and I have grown more in love with Jesus through them.

Grandma has modeled for me what it means to love Jesus and to serve Him with passion and energy. My life has been greatly enriched by her, and I thank God that she has been part of my life. One day she will hear the words of her Savior: "Well done, good and faithful servant." I can only pray that someday I will hear the same.

2

Courage for Life's Reality

Joanne Cornelius

How does one write an appropriate introduc-
*tion to the story of two of the best friends I have ever had or will
have? I am not sure and pray that my words will do justice to
the incredible relationship that I have had with both Jack and
Joanne Samad. These are two people that my wife, Sharon, and I
have shared life with. We have served together, worked together,
laughed and cried together, and have prayed for and with one
another. The words "friendship" or even "fellowship" do not tell
all that needs to be told. Jack and Joanne are people whom Sharon and I simply have loved very deeply.*

*Our relationship started soon after they joined College Hill
Presbyterian Church in 1976. We were all active in ministry at
College Hill, and our paths crossed often. Then, in 1980, Jack
was diagnosed with cancer. Sharon and I joined many others in
praying for complete healing. Despite the reality that the Lord
did not answer our prayers as we had asked, He gave Jack twenty-eight more years of life—and what a life it was. Through all
the pain, cancer treatments, and many setbacks, Jack learned to
live every day as a gift from the Lord. He was an inspiration to
all who knew him.*

Eventually Jack and Joanne both joined the staff of the National Coalition Against Pornography, so we then had the opportunity to serve together in a great ministry addressing one of the most challenging issues facing the world and the church. This partnership brought the amazing skills, energy, and commitment to Jesus that they had lived out. Joanne would say that Jack and I would argue loudly and often, but at the end of the day we were absolutely together in our commitment to Jesus and the National Coalition Against Pornography. Joanne demonstrated her skills in loving people and calling forth their gifts and resources for building the Kingdom of God.

Joanne's story is one of faith, trust, and love of God through both the good and the difficult times. What a blessing it has been to see their two children following Jesus in the footsteps of their parents. In 2013, Joanne surprised us with her marriage to Carl Cornelius. He is a really good man who loves Christ and Joanne deeply. God has blessed again!

This book could not possibly have been written without Joanne's story. Her life is truly a demonstration of how ordinary people serve our extraordinary God.

Joanne's Story

I was born in Cincinnati, Ohio, in 1954, the youngest of three girls. My sisters were ten and fifteen when I came into the world, so in many ways I am like an only child.

I grew up in a crazy extended household. My grandma and grandpa Miller lived upstairs from us, and my grandma was famous for taking in anyone who needed a place to stay. Rooms were always being shuffled around, and I never remember a time when someone was not at home. Grandma invited one of her friends to stay with her while she recuperated from a fall. That woman became my godmother and precious Aunt Laura, and she lived in our home until she passed fifty-three years later, when I was twenty-one.

My mom and dad were not churchgoers other than at Easter, but my grandma Miller was the godliest woman I have ever known. She taught me to pray when I was very young—so young that I don't remember ever going to sleep without reciting "Now I lay me down to sleep" and asking God to bless everyone I knew.

When I was in elementary school, I always felt out of place because I never attended Sunday school and all of my friends did. In God's providence, when I was eleven years old, I started going to church with my sister and her husband, and I was confirmed in a United Methodist church when I was twelve. I loved confirmation class, and when it came time for the examination, I received a perfect score. The pastor interviewed us individually, and when he asked if I died why should God let me into heaven, my immediate answer was "because Jesus died for me." I still remember that day like it was yesterday. On Confirmation Sunday, I was asked to lead the congregation in prayer, and my grandma Miller helped me write out a beautiful prayer. Even though it wasn't all my words, my heart was bursting with thankfulness that Sunday.

My Relationship with Jack

I met my future husband in kindergarten! He became a "special" friend when I was thirteen. We were both the youngest in our families by a long shot, and it didn't take long for us to become very dependent on each other. Our parents were out and about most of the time, so we leaned on each other many times, and in many ways, he was my one secure relationship. We both knew the Lord, but during our teenage years our life with Him often resembled a seesaw. I especially experienced many ups and downs with my relationship with the Lord. In high school, I was very involved at my church, but I'm not sure my motives were always clear. In some ways it was the best way I could rebel against my parents. I loved them very much, but I resented the fact that they were never very present in my life.

Eventually, I decided I wanted to go to a Christian college, knowing that would go over like a lead balloon with my parents. I was right—they were not supportive, so I decided not to go to college at all. It was a decision I deeply regretted for years, and the Lord showed me often that decision was based on my pride and resentment. I was forced to live with the consequences of my stubbornness. Eventually I was able to go to school for a year and a half when my children were in elementary school, and I am so grateful that the Lord showed me that my worth doesn't depend on anything other than my relationship with Him.

We made it through our bumpy journey of high school, and Jack proposed to me in January 1974, one month before my twentieth birthday and ten months after Grandma Miller passed. We married in August 1975, Jack's senior year in college. I was ecstatic! We moved to Richmond, Kentucky, where Jack finished his last year, and I was able to land a very good job as Administrative Assistant to the Director of the College of Music. I loved that job. After being in Richmond for about three months without thinking much about church, Jack and I woke up one Sunday and both knew something was missing. We needed to find a church.

We often found ourselves coming to Cincinnati for the weekend to visit family, so we started going to the church at which we were married. On Easter Sunday, we invited a friend to come to church with us, and she suggested we visit her church on the next Sunday. In April 1976, we visited College Hill Presbyterian Church. Both of us were forever changed and recommitted our lives to Christ on the same day.

The Challenge of Sickness

We desired to start our family, and being part of a committed church community was just what we needed. We tried for several years without success and three years later began taking infertility drugs. I became pregnant but miscarried early. After a dream Jack had about Abraham and Sarah, the Lord made it clear to us that if we waited for His timing instead of taking things into our own hands, He would provide. Six months after we lost our baby, Jack was diagnosed with Hodgkin's lymphoma. He was twenty-six and I was twenty-five. We were devastated. Jack had just landed a contract in his newly established videotape business, we were finally in the market for a home, and we thought things were just getting started for us. The Lord, in His wisdom, had other plans.

Treatment for cancer was much different in those days—no CT scans, no lasers to pinpoint radiation. After a very painful staging surgery and three months of radiation, Jack was skinny, weak, and badly burned. The one person who made me feel secure was discouraged and pretty much wanted to check out. I was scared to death. It was then that my life verse became Philippians 4:6–7: "Do not be anxious about anything, but in every situation, by prayer and petition, with thanksgiving, present your requests to God. And the peace of God, which transcends all understanding, will guard your hearts and your minds in Christ Jesus." To this day it is the first verse that comes to my mind when I face difficult circumstances. It is etched on my heart (and etched on my headstone!).

Jack later shared how he felt when he thought about suicide—and when the Holy Spirit nudged him and lifted him up. It was amazing. I remember one day thinking he would never survive the treatment and then watching him being filled with a determination to live life to the fullest, and that he certainly did. I learned so much from him about never taking time for granted. Even though the coming years were hard, Jack made sure we had many, many joyous and fun moments.

Jack finished treatment in November 1980. Miraculously, without any medication, we became pregnant with our son, Jacob, in January 1981, and then were blessed with a daughter, Christy, in 1984. The doctors were shocked, but we believed God's promise and tried our best to put our future in God's hands.

The radiation certainly cured the Hodgkin's lymphoma, but it was very hard on Jack's body, and over the next twenty-nine years he suffered from its results. His immune system was compromised, so infection was not uncommon, but the most devastating effect was on his heart because the radiation was not pinpointed by laser. After a pacemaker, biventricular defibrillator, many stent insertions, a bout with sepsis, and many other serious side effects, he was diagnosed with lung cancer in December 2007. The Lord was gracious and took him home on May 22, 2008.

Jack was in the hospital at least a couple of times every year after he was diagnosed in 1979—twelve of which we didn't think he would survive. Every time he was in surgery I would go to the chapel and pray through Psalm 103: "Praise the LORD, my soul; all my inmost being, praise His holy name. Praise the LORD, my soul, and forget not all His benefits." I can't tell you how many times peace would fill my heart, even though at times it felt like it was breaking.

I had three men in my life in whom I put my security. My dad, who passed when I was thirty, four years after Jack was diagnosed; my brother-in-law, Jim, who I knew would take care of me if Jack would die; and Jack.

Jim was diagnosed with cancer and passed within two years, the same month we found out about Jack's lung cancer. It was crystal clear the Lord was telling me that the only security we have in our lives is to put our faith and trust in Him. Psalm 73:26 became very real to me: "My flesh and my heart may fail, but God is the strength of my heart and my portion forever."

It was a rough time from the world's perspective. From December 2007 to December 2008 our family lost Jim, Jack, and my sister, Nancy, and her husband, Joe. My sweet daughter-in-law, Amy, the wife of my son, Jacob, had three miscarriages; and we were heartbroken. It was very different because for the first time I had to depend on the Lord without my life partner by my side. I fell in love with Jack when I was so young that I couldn't remember a time when he wasn't there! It's funny, though—I could feel the experiences of my past cheering me on. It was time to either sink or swim.

New Blessings

In 2011, God surprised me! I had been praying about my future, knowing I needed something or someone outside my children. Of course, they were absolutely amazing, and my son and his wife, Amy, gave me two beautiful grandchildren, Jack and Audrey. But I knew I could not put my security in Jacob or Christy and that I needed to be open to what my future might hold. In March, I met Carl Cornelius. It makes me laugh when I think of how the Lord knew what I needed—someone who grew up in the same neighborhood, knew Jesus, went to the same high school, had tons of mutual friends, and grew up about a mile from where I did, yet we had never met!

Carl and I were married in March 2013. He and I now share a family of five children and their families, which include eleven grandchildren, and life is full. One thing I've learned through all of this is that there are challenging days, but how we respond to difficulties and who we trust for our ultimate happiness makes all the difference in the outcome.

Jack and I had opportunities to share our testimony many times. Jack would always say, "I wouldn't have chosen this road, but I don't know which part of it I would give up." Isn't that true? The Lord teaches us so much through life's experiences.

I'm thankful that He didn't just leave me to wallow in the past when Jack passed. Don't get me wrong, there isn't a day that passes that I don't miss him and wonder what life would be like if he were still here. And there are some sad moments in the midst of joy. My beautiful daughter, Christy, married David in 2018, and boy did we miss Jack on her wedding day—but oh how I've learned that our joy does not depend on our circumstances but finding it in the one who makes it possible to breathe and laugh and cry. He cares for me, and He cares for you! First Peter 5:7 says, "Cast all your anxiety on him because he cares for you." I will tell you I have experienced His caring hand more times than I can count.

None of us knows how long we have on this planet, but something I hold on to is that if bad news comes our way, nothing has changed—we just have more information. The security we have in knowing we are going to see Jesus face-to-face someday is all we need to know. We are not yet at the home for which we were created. Until we are, God promises to never leave or forsake us no matter how messy life gets. I give Him thanks for all of my life. I look forward to more grandchildren! After all these years I am still a work in progress, and I am thankful He has shown me His great faithfulness and mercy.

3

Restoring Marriages

Al and Linda Cole

I first heard of Al and Linda from Rick Kardos, *the New England director for pureHope (formerly the National Coalition Against Pornography and also the National Coalition for the Protection of Children and Families). Rick had invited them to share their journey at an Iron Sharpens Iron men's conference. Their transparency and giftedness helped couples rebuild trust and love in their marriages.*

Soon after Rick Kardos had them speak, I met them at another conference. I was immediately struck by their commitment to marriage and to restoring the broken. They knew that God hates divorce, and because of their personal journey they were being effective in ministering to others. Their book, The Shadow Christian, was published in 2005, and we started using it at pureHope.

In 2006, Al and Linda started inviting me to join them at church events and conferences in greater Atlanta. God opened many doors for ministry there, and we became closer personally and professionally. As these doors were opened more and more couples came forward, acknowledging that they were struggling. Pornography use was rampant even among Christians in the middle of the Bible belt. The opportunities were amazing but at the same time overwhelming. More had to be done, so in 2008 pureHope hired Al to be its full-time director of the Atlanta office.

Over the years God has used this couple to bless many individuals and couples. They have found that no situation is too dire for God to restore and rebuild. If couples are genuinely committed to Christ and to their marriages, God has shown them that He can do amazing things. Not all the stories have an "And they lived happily ever after" ending, but Al and Linda remain committed to the calling that God has placed on their lives. They are another example of God using ordinary people to do His extraordinary work. To God be all the glory.

Al and Linda's Story

Al

My mom was one of nine children, and we were raised in the Catholic Church in New Orleans. Our whole family went to church regularly, but I had no personal relationship with God. I attended Catholic schools through high school, but for me, God was very distant. I didn't come to a meaningful faith until the age of fifty-three, and it grew out of a significant life crisis.

Linda

Growing up, I went to church regularly, but my parents went to different churches, my mom to the Baptist church and my dad to an Episcopalian one. My parents had a very difficult marriage, and my father started drinking. I was the youngest of three girls, and my father favored me over my sisters because he always wanted a boy and I was a good athlete. I was active as a teenager in youth group, and most of my friends were in the church. My mom read Scripture with me regularly.

Al and I had first marriages that failed, mine because of physical abuse. Al and I dated for two years and were married in 1980. In 1985, we moved from New Orleans to Washington, DC, and we joined the Methodist church. I continued in my faith journey but was still distant from God. Outsiders saw our marriage as "made in heaven." But this was only an outward appearance.

The Discovery

Al

Linda discovered that I had an addiction to pornography in November 2001. I thought I had hidden the porn on my computer—but one night when she was doing an innocent Web search, some of the images popped up. When she confronted me, my initial response was denial. At that time there was not a lot of understanding about sexual brokenness and addiction. Fortunately, at Linda's insistence, I went through a four-day intensive sexual integrity program and later began to see a counselor regularly.

Linda

I did not know why all this was happening, but I certainly did not accept Al's behavior. My heart was broken, but I was confident enough to realize that I was not to blame. I didn't know what to do, but I did insist that Al get help. I was pleased and encouraged that he wanted help. I was in the same position as Ruth Graham when she was asked whether she ever considered divorcing Billy. Her response was, "No ... but I did think of murder a few times."

By the time I discovered Al's addiction, we already had three beautiful children. Our daughter was seventeen and had just entered college. Our fifteen-year-old son was away at boarding school, and our oldest was living in Maryland. Al and I agreed not to tell them about his addiction until he was well on the way to recovery. After a year of counseling, we decided that Al should write them a letter and read it to them, which he later said was one of the hardest things he ever had to do. In the letter he acknowledged that he was not perfect and that his use of pornography was destructive and sinful, and he assured them that he was getting help. We also assured our kids that we were committed to staying together and working to rebuild our marriage.

From Wholeness to Serving

Several years later, as Al got healthier and our marriage became stronger, we began to minister to other couples who were going through a similar struggle. We aren't licensed counselors, but we drew richly from our personal experience and partnered with professional Christian counselors. At the center of our helping others is showing the genuine love of Jesus for both husbands and wives, and how God will provide the necessary grace, if both partners are willing to do the work.

In our journey of helping other couples, we have learned that three principles must be in place for real progress to be made. All three of the principles are based on the power and truth of God's Word.

The first key principle is a mutual commitment to Jesus Christ as Lord and Savior. Without that there is no real hope. Second, we demand that both the husband and wife be 100 percent committed to restoring their marriage and relationship. Third, they must recognize that this is a long journey, without a specific timeline. These couples are in their current situation, not because of a one-time, immediate problem, but through pornography use that has developed over many years, often decades, of brokenness. Next, we want them to know that there is real hope for restoration both individually and as a couple. Finally, both parties must understand that healing will require significant change in the way they think about love, commitment, marriage, and honesty.

The Scriptures are central to our ministry, and there are several significant passages that we find helpful in our personal ministry and in helping others:

> I tell you in the same way that there will be more rejoicing in heaven over one sinner who repents than over ninety-nine righteous persons who do not need to repent. (Luke 15:7)

This one was very important to me (Al) personally when I was struggling soon after discovery.

> We are hard pressed on every side, but not crushed; perplexed, but not in despair; persecuted, but not abandoned; struck down, but not destroyed. (2 Cor. 4:8–9)

This one speaks to the endurance necessary on the journey from brokenness to wholeness.

> Do not merely listen to the word, and so deceive yourselves. Do what it says. (James 1:22).

I (Al) use this to remind guys that words alone are not enough.

> Yet this I call to mind and therefore I have
> hope:
> Because of the LORD's great love we are not
> consumed, for his compassions never fail.
> They are new every morning; great is your
> faithfulness. (Lam. 3:21–23)

Again, a verse that reassures us that He loves us and will never forsake us.

> But he said to me, "My grace is sufficient for you, for my power is made perfect in weakness." Therefore I will boast all the more gladly about my weaknesses, so that Christ's power may rest on me. (2 Cor. 12:9)

Linda and I always close our testimony with this verse. It speaks to the humility God desires from us.

The thief comes only to steal and kill and destroy; I have come that they may have life, and have it to the full. (John 10:10)

We use this to remind couples that the abundant life that Jesus promised is attainable.

In our ministry we talk about the big lies that pornography users believe and tell their spouses. The first lie is that this is not a big deal. It is just me and the computer. The second lie is that this was the first and only time I have ever looked at pornography. The third and most devastating lie is that my porn use is her fault, implying that the spouse is not loving enough, accepting enough, sexy enough, or beautiful enough for me.

Our ministry began in July 2005 when our book, *The Shadow Christian,* was published. This book tells our story of how a marriage that appeared to be solid and strong was actually in desperate need of healing. That fall, we were contacted by Rick Kardos, who was the New England director for the National Coalition for the Protection of Children and Families. He asked us whether we would come to New England to speak at an Iron Sharpens Iron men's conference in Hartford, Connecticut. Two months later, he invited us to be part of a two-day church training session in Boston led by Ted Roberts, founder of Pure Desire Ministries. At both, we were greatly encouraged by the openness of so many in attendance. Soon after, Al began to work with men struggling to break free from the bondage of pornography.

Al

Our ministry expanded when I joined the staff of the National Coalition for the Protection of Children and Families in 2008 as Director of the Atlanta office. We received numerous requests from churches to speak about our own experience and share what we had learned. Two years later, we were invited to lead off a weekend couples' intensive by giving our testimony and taking questions for twenty minutes. As it turned out, we answered questions for more than an hour from the seven couples there. These were couples who had been in counseling for at least a year, yet were hungry to learn what a successful recovery looked like in the flesh.

On the drive back home, Linda and I realized that there was a significant piece of the recovery puzzle that was missing that we could provide. That's when we started groups for Christian married couples who wanted real help. We have focused our ministry on working with couples in which both the husband and wife are involved and committed to move toward recovery from brokenness. I work primarily with the husbands, while Linda works with the wives. Both spouses need hope and encouragement in their walk with Christ, and practical strategies to improve their relationship. We wish we could say that everyone we worked with has been a success story, but that is not true.

Some Stories from Al and Linda's Ministry

Story 1

Mary was six months pregnant with their first child when she suddenly began to cry during a group session for couples whose marriages had been damaged by pornography, affairs, and other forms of sexual sin. She was sitting next to another woman in the group, feeling unloved because her husband, John, was out of town instead of being with her like the husbands of the other three wives. This was not the first time John had missed a session. After all the couples were gone, Linda and Al both shared their doubts about whether this marriage would survive.

The following week, John made arrangements to be available for the group even though he had to be out of town again. When Mary sat down, she put her smartphone down beside her, and there was John on FaceTime. Everyone had a good laugh about it, but for the next two hours, John was present with Mary, fully engaged and able to listen and respond to what the group was doing. This seemingly small, caring gesture by John meant the world to Mary, and it was a turning point in their relationship. John continued to honor his commitments, which is a vital component to healing a broken relationship. He did so for the remainder of the group and beyond. A few years later, they welcomed their third child into the world, and their marriage is still going strong.

Story 2

Carl and Katherine had been separated for a year when they were referred to us. Over the twenty-plus years of their marriage, Carl had engaged in multiple affairs and Katherine had given him a number of chances to repair the damage each time. But the most recent betrayal had pushed her to the point where she finally asked him to move out. Carl and Katherine made steady progress in their couples' group, and God extended the grace they both needed as they worked toward healing. There were glimmers of hope along the way as Carl and Katherine seemed to be drawing closer to God and rekindling the spark that originally brought them together.

But toward the end of the twenty-six-week group, Carl announced that he was planning a weeklong beach vacation with two male friends. After Al warned him that this would not be a good environment for him and would send the wrong message to Katherine, Carl reluctantly chose not to go. Unfortunately, the incident raised serious doubts in Katherine's mind about Carl's judgment, doubts she was unable to shake. When the group ended a few weeks later, she decided she was not willing to risk being hurt again and would be okay living on her own, even as she acknowledged that Carl had grown spiritually over the previous six months. Despite our best efforts and much prayer, their relationship ended in divorce.

Story 3

Al's first meeting with Mike lasted ninety minutes, during which Mike largely minimized the degree to which his extramarital sexual activity had hurt his wife, Marsha. Toward the end of the conversation, however, Mike slowly began to acknowledge the severity of what he had done to her. A few days later, against Al's advice, Mike was overcome with guilt and disclosed to Marsha additional infidelities, which she was not prepared to hear. The next day, Linda met with the heartbroken young woman to offer her counsel and comfort, having experienced the same feelings of betrayal herself many years ago, even though the details were different. After their conversation, Marsha agreed to accompany Mike to a session with Linda and Al, at which time Marsha pressed Mike into revealing more incidents.

At this point, the situation appeared hopeless, but Marsha's anger was tempered by Mike's tears, and she was deeply moved by her husband's sincere regret and his promise to do whatever it would take to make things right with her and with God. One of the things Mike agreed to do was to see a counselor Al recommended. For the next several weeks, Al was in contact with Mike virtually every day. In time, Marsha joined Mike with the counselor. Eventually Mike disclosed the rest of his sins to her in the presence of the counselor. As difficult as that was for Marsha, this time she was prepared. Having seen positive signs of change in Mike, she was willing to give him another chance to prove himself. Two years later they are progressing nicely.

4

From Shame to Wholeness

John Comstock

Through the Religious Alliance Against *Pornography, I have had the privilege of working with some of the top leaders of the Church of the Nazarene. I have found them to be among the most humble and godly men and women I have had the privilege of meeting. Through the Religious Alliance against Pornography I met John Comstock, who has turned out to be an effective leader and a trusted friend. He has been a prayer partner and it has been a blessing to follow Jesus together.*

John has led the Religious Alliance against Pornography in producing training webinars that have helped thousands. He is committed to the holiness of God's people and has a clear understanding of the destructive impact of pornography. John has helped recruit a number of strong presenters for the webinars and was one of the presenters of the webinar focused on guilt and shame. His understanding of shame comes from deep personal experiences, not just from an academic perspective. John's story is one that highlights a commitment to Christ at a very young age yet shows the challenges of living this out. His story is very real and genuine. You will be blessed by it.

John's Story

I was born in Fort Scott, Kansas, in 1974. I have two older sisters. Mom and Dad are still alive. Mom was raised Nazarene. She walked away from God, but believe it or not, our mailman was a Nazarene, and he turned out to be the key to her return to church. So I was raised in a Christian home. God is so surprising! When I was nine years old, my dad was called to the pastorate in the Church of the Nazarene.

I was very active in church and made a personal commitment to Christ at the age of six. During that time, I was in and around people of faith and was spiritually enriched and very active in my faith. I began preaching at age twelve. I started in ministry while I was in high school leading weekend revivals, and I even did pulpit supply at a church for three months. During these early years, I saw God move in powerful and amazing ways.

I went to MidAmerica Nazarene University, a school in Olathe, Kansas, and graduated in 2000 with a degree in ministry. I met my wife, Amy, at school, and we married between our junior and senior years. God has blessed us with three children, two beautiful girls and a wonderful son.

The Challenges in the Call

Despite my early Christian commitment and years in ministry, I found myself fighting a vocational call to ministry. Despite this struggle, God continued to open doors. Friends introduced me to the Mapping Center for Evangelism, which was founded jointly by Bill Bright of Campus

Crusade and the Southern Baptist Convention. During this time (1999–2003), I had the privilege of working with many pastors. God was orchestrating His call on my life. At the worst time, the Mapping Center ran out of money, and, I was let go. This was a personal disaster.

Many men and women who are serving the Lord in full-time ministry experience great joy and peace, but that was not my experience. I suffered from anxiety and obsessive-compulsive behavior. At the worst of my struggles, I was only sleeping three to four hours a night.

I worked for the Billy Graham Organization in preparation for their crusade in Kansas City in 2004. Then, in 2005, I began working as the continuing lay training coordinator for the international headquarters of the Church of the Nazarene. In my role as continuing lay training coordinator, I manage a website designed for the laity, DiscipleshipPlace.org. The website has educational courses and resources designed to provide ministry training and theological coherence. I facilitate webinars to educate the laity on various topics covering ministry training and discipleship. I also do workshops and speak on how shame affects our relationship with God and how to heal our broken image of God.

The work done in creating these resources is often initiated by listening to the needs shared by pastors and laity. In one such case, I recall a phone call I received at the office in which a mom was sharing about her process of grieving. Her son, an avid hunter, was anticipating an extended hunting trip with his dad. As she was talking with her son about this excursion, she asked what kind of food she could prepare for them to take on the trip. As he shared his menu of choice to her, she began working in the kitchen, and within a matter of minutes, she recalls being terrified by the sound of a gunshot. The initial reaction to this jarring sound was one of anger as she thought, *How could he have let that gun go off in the house?* As she walked into the bedroom to see what happened, she was horrified to find her son lying dead in a pool of blood. The day she called the office was one year to the day of this incident, and through a wave of tears she shared that there were several in her church encouraging her to "get over it and move on." It was at that moment that a decision was made to have an expert on grief, Dr. Harold Ivan Smith, do a training on the grieving process.

Another ministry opportunity came to me in 2014 when I became the official representative of the Church of the Nazarene to the Religious Alliance against Pornography. The Religious Alliance against Pornography is an interfaith organization focused exclusively on the negative effects of pornography. My role has been to host Religious Alliance against Pornography's live webinars, which have covered such subjects as pornography and addiction, helping parents lead their children in our overly sexualized culture, pornography and its relationship to sex trafficking, and helping the church address this vitally important issue. Thousands of individuals and church leaders have been trained and discipled through these webinars. I was even given the privilege of being one of the presenters on the topic of pornography and shame.

A Turn in the Road

On the way to the office in 2015, I received a call that changed the trajectory of my work. Assuming this was a typical call from my father, I answered by saying, "Hey, Dad, what's up?" My dad immediately responded, "Not good. Scott just hung himself." It was in that instant of hearing of my brother-in-law's death that God spoke and invited me to engage in ministry work that would help people heal from their woundedness. This has led to the subsequent work in the area of shame and healing. This experience has led me to see more clearly what shame and brokenness, even among Christians, is all about.

I have committed myself to help others confront shame and have spoken frequently on this topic. This comes not just from the experience of my brother-in-law but from my own life experience. I have found when speaking about this issue that many people come forward to share their shame and to ask for help. Many deeply committed Christians who experience this shame wonder where God is. He feels so absent.

In my ministry, some cognitively know a great deal about God but struggle to have a sense of His presence. Over the years, I have begun to see that information about God is not enough. The key to wholeness and holiness is a deep heart connection to the living God. Vulnerability to God and others, which includes confession and repentance, must be a regular component of daily Christian living. Shame is the dam that blocks the sense of God's presence.

Christians often do not trust emotions. This causes us to suppress or dismiss them, but the emotions are still there and often are causing pain at very deep levels. This leads to all kinds of ways to self-medicate.

In my calling to help people understand and deal with their emotions, I have used a helpful training exercise. I ask people to close their eyes and imagine that Jesus is urgently looking for them. Next, I ask them to imagine that He is standing directly in front of them. The key question I ask is, "How do you feel in the presence of Jesus?" Often, people share their fear and anxiety that Jesus is so close. I help them see that such feelings are likely expressions of shame. When people go through this kind of exercise, it helps them become aware of the emotional sense of shame in their lives. This is often the starting place of healing.

At a recent retreat, I led the group through this exercise. In the group debrief time, one person shared he didn't know how difficult it was going to be to look Jesus into the eyes. He confessed, "I have not shared this with anyone, but I do not even want to live." Whether it is a person struggling in life without hope or the church leader coming up to confess a struggle with shame while weeping, the awareness of how prevalent shame is in our churches and our society is hard to dismiss. The healing presence of the risen Christ is needed.

This issue presented itself again one evening when I received a phone call asking me to come to the home of some friends who had an urgent need. When I arrived, there were several adults present in the room. It was filled with tension. The young man who was the source of the tension had earlier that day threatened his dad. In the conversation with the young man, I learned that his father had abused him for years.

Everyone was asking, especially the young man, "Where is God in this situation?" He acknowledged that he had indeed threatened his dad. I had the young man close his eyes and relive this experience. He was able to share what happened when he made the threat. I asked him whether he could see Jesus in this place. Of course, his answer was "No." I assured him that Jesus was there. He replied, "If Jesus were there, He would be very angry." I responded that wasn't like Jesus. Instead, Jesus reaches out with compassion and love. It became clear this young man was desperate for forgiveness, but he was unable to receive it. This inability to receive forgiveness was the result of deep shame. And of course, here we have the great blockage. God's loving presence doesn't come through. That day this young man was able to find Jesus in the darkness of his inner rage.

The answer to being loved by God is the proper understanding of God. God is love, and Scripture teaches that we only love God because God first loved us. A healthy, orthodox view of God leads to freedom, including emotional freedom from the inside out!

In my spiritual journey and ministry, I have attempted to be led by the Word of God. His Word brings the grace, love, forgiveness, and wholeness that He promises into our lives. In dealing with shame, brokenness and guilt, we must remain committed to God's truth.

Living by and in the Word of God

I believe that the entire Bible is God's inspired, authoritative, and infallible Word for all of us. Several passages have been particularly helpful to me and to those I serve.

John 1 is where the gospel begins. It presents the love of God in Christ as our Redeemer, Healer, and Savior. Jesus is our Lord and King. Understanding this gives hope and healing in all of our broken places.

The essence of the Christian faith is the uniqueness of Jesus (John 14:6–20). He is not a way but *the* way to the Father. He is the incarnate Word, which is the truth of God in human flesh. He is life itself, and those who follow Him are blessed with His promise of the abundant life, which He shares with us in John 10:10–11.

In Ephesians 3:14–21, Paul invokes the love of God the Father, asking that the love of Christ be brought from heaven by the power of the Holy Spirit into the hearts of all believers. Through this prayer, Paul teaches us to pray for spiritual power to know the expansiveness of spiritual love that is bigger than we can even say, think, or imagine. When the love of Christ fills us, we move from being empty to being full. We move from mere conceptual knowledge to rich experiential knowledge. This is the journey to wholeness.

5

Love God, His People, and His Word

Jerry Kirk

My relationship with Jerry Kirk began in *1968, when he led a renewal weekend at the Newton Presbyterian Church in Newton, Massachusetts. This was during my second year at the Harvard Business School. That weekend Jerry preached on the Lordship of Christ and the possibility of a personal relationship with Jesus. I had never heard such a message and at the end of that weekend I gave my life to Christ. So Jerry was the person who shared the gospel for the first time in a way that I could hear it.*

He became my pastor at College Hill Presbyterian Church in Cincinnati, Ohio. He discipled me and hundreds of others. My wife, Sharon, and I were in a small community group with Jerry, his wife, Patty and two other couples.

In 1990 Jerry asked whether I would pray about leaving the business world and enter into full-time vocational ministry. After much prayer I decided that God was calling me to do just that. This started a journey of serving the Lord together in ministry, which continues to this very day. We started serving the

National Coalition Against Pornography (now known as pure-Hope). After our service at pureHope we have continued to minister together through the Prayer Covenant, which is discipling adults and children around the world in a life-changing, lifelong discipline of prayer.

Jerry and I have practiced for over fifty years the principle "iron sharpens iron" (Proverbs 27:17). We have opened our lives to each other at the deepest levels and have practiced what it means to genuinely hold one another accountable in our service to Jesus.

Despite the incredible personal relationship that I have with Jerry, that is not why he is included in this book. He is included first of all as an example of someone who came from a non-Christian home but was called by God to a lifetime of service. He became the senior pastor and served College Hill Presbyterian Church from 1967 until 1986. Over those years he called God's people to grow in their service and love of Jesus. He gathered a strong pastoral leadership team which discipled hundreds of Jesus' followers to use their gifts in service and ministry. He preached and taught around the country about the love of Jesus and calling people to get out of the pews and to serve their Lord.

In some ways Jerry should be considered a revolutionary. He started a revolution of discipleship at College Hill Presbyterian Church and fought the battle for biblical standards for those seeking ordination within his denomination. His revolutionary ways continued in leading the battle against pornography and then at the age of eighty-two he started the ministry of the Prayer Covenant.

Everyone who meets Jerry immediately knows two things — first, that he loves Jesus, and second, that he loves you. This is truly a grace gift from God that very few people have. This is the mark of a disciple who is seeking to follow our Lord and to serve for His glory.

Jerry's Story

I was born in 1931 in Seattle. My family was non-Christian so we rarely went to church. There was great emphasis on character, integrity, and self-discipline in my home. I could see these in both my father and my mother. Dad had been a Rose Bowl football player for the University of Washington. He maintained his interest in athletics as he coached high school football, baseball, and basketball. After I left for seminary, my father served two terms in the House of Representatives for the state of Washington before going into county politics. My mother was also politically active as a legislator for six terms.

As a boy I loved to gamble. I would bet with my friends on anything from the weather to a sports competition. I bought a car at age fourteen without my parents' knowledge and I paid $50 for it from my gambling proceeds. I had some spiritual interest at that point and I bought the car so that I could go to church. My church attendance didn't last long, as my father found out and put a stop to it. Further, he demanded that I sell the car.

At that time, we were living in Pasco, Washington, because my father was a naval officer during World War II. I learned to drive a truck on my grandfather's farm even though I was only fourteen. This was a difficult time in my life. My parents were very busy. I often skipped school and got in a good deal of trouble.

During my senior year in high school we moved back to Seattle. I was on both the basketball and tennis teams.

My participation and achievements in sports were the direct result of the modeling and influence of my parents. That year I was introduced to Ad Sewell, the director for Young Life in the Northwest. He invited me to attend a Young Life camp in Colorado at Star Ranch.

Initially I declined the invitation because I wanted to continue my tennis competition. My tennis coach, however, encouraged me to go. I also found out that Mike McCutcheon, one of the outstanding basketball players in the entire city of Seattle was attending the camp and he asked me to come with him. That quickly changed my mind. I went to the camp not out of any spiritual interest at this point but because I wanted to hang around Mike. My attitude at camp was guarded. I even got into a fight with several others.

Jesus Welcomes Me Home

Later in the week I heard the message of the cross. I was deeply touched and committed my life to Jesus. Mike McCutcheon was already a committed believer before going to the camp. He learned of my commitment to Christ and immediately took me under his wing. When I told him that I had committed my life to Christ at the evening meeting, he said to me, "Do you know that that means?"

I said, "No, but I want to learn."

Mike responded, "That means you get to meet with Jesus at the beginning of every day and you get to live with Him all day long." Wow! That brief conversation set the direction and priority of my life for the rest of life.

While attending the University of Washington, I continued to be active in both Young Life and with the

Navigators. I led Bible studies at the University of Washington and was challenged to start a Young Life Club in Bothell, a suburb of Seattle. My first attempt at starting a club for high school students did not go well. As I spoke with the Young Life leaders about the poor response, I was told, "You need to pay the price to be heard." I got the message both for developing that Young Life group and for experiences that followed! As I began to invite kids, God started opening doors. It was exciting! Within six months there were 125 kids coming.

While working intensively with Young Life, I also continued my participation on both the basketball and tennis teams and did well. Our basketball team went to the Final Four. However, I did not go, as I had left the team the year before to focus exclusively on tennis, as I thought my future was to be a professional tennis player. God in His wisdom had other plans.

After college, I planned on studying at Fuller Theological Seminary in Pasadena, California. However, my pastor, Cliff Smith, had been called to Mount Lebanon Presbyterian Church in Pittsburgh. He wanted me to work with him at that church, but I said no because I was already committed to Fuller and was also to lead the Glendale Young Life club. But Cliff was persistent and eventually went to Jim Rayburn, the founder and President of Young Life. Jim called and urged me to start a new Young Life club in Pittsburgh working with Cliff Smith. After all this, I felt called to go to Pittsburgh.

Life Change and Ministry in Pittsburgh

I met my wife, Patty, while I was in seminary. She had graduated from Moody Bible Institute and was called to youth ministry at a Pittsburgh church. Our first date was to go to a high school football game so I could meet students for founding of a Young Life club. I didn't want to go into the game when it started, as I thought we could get in free at halftime. Turns out I was wrong. Since I didn't have any money, Patty had to buy our tickets. Despite this rocky start, we dated for four years and then got married when I graduated from seminary in 1956.

As I started Young Life in Pittsburgh, I took students to Young Life camps and was delighted to see their lives transformed as they became involved in church youth groups around the city.

My first church after graduating from seminary was Mt. Lebanon United Presbyterian Church in Mt. Lebanon, Pennsylvania, where I was the associate pastor for youth ministry. I left Mt. Lebanon to become pastor at New Wilmington United Presbyterian Church in New Wilmington, Pennsylvania.

God's Call to College Hill Presbyterian Church

While I was pastoring there, I was contacted by the pastor search committee from College Hill Presbyterian Church in Cincinnati. I said no twice, but thankfully they continued to pursue me. Finally, I said yes in 1967. I arrived as the new pastor in November. I had often felt inadequate and over my head in ministering to 650 Presbyterians in my prior congregation. You can imagine how I felt when called to lead a congregation of 2,300.

My first Friday night there, the middle-aged couples group, called Questors, was meeting at the church to share a meal and hear the personal story of Bob Scheck, an executive with Procter & Gamble. At forty-five, he was leaving the business world, going to seminary, and becoming a pastor.

It was an amazing evening with wonderful food, lots of fun and a warm and wholesome fellowship. Bob's witness of coming to Christ, his influence among his business associates and his sense of call to ministry were contagious. The whole time I was listening to him, I was talking to God inwardly: "Lord, surely you don't want me to do something crazy. Give me your wisdom. Guide me in what to say. This is my first meeting as their pastor, and their first exposure to me apart from the pulpit. Lord, this is a sophisticated congregation. Help me get acquainted gradually and have the opportunity to get to know them as persons and learn their names, etc., etc., etc. Please use me."

Bob finished, and it was time for me to speak. I told them how pleased I was to be part of their fellowship for this special evening and how I had come to know the Lord and experience Christ in ways similar to Bob Scheck. I told them how much I respected him for his decision to leave the business world at forty-five and to pay for three years of graduate education at seminary while supporting his family, knowing all the time that at the end he would receive a salary that would be dramatically less than what he was making at Procter & Gamble.

Then I decided to have a Presbyterian altar call. Do you know what that is? It is subtle. It is low-key. This is what I said: "I can tell that we have been blessed tonight. God has met us in this place. Some of us might want to stay around and talk about it. If that is true for you, come back into the parlor fifteen minutes after we break, and we will discuss our response to what we have heard."

Seventeen people came into the parlor. We put the chairs into a circle, and I turned to the person on my left. "Lois, what led you to come into the parlor, and what are your thoughts about what we have heard from Bob? Let's go around the circle with each one of you sharing your thoughts. When we are done, we will end our evening." Over two hours later we had heard from everyone. The testimonies and sharing were deep, personal, and life-giving.

In closing our time, I said to them, "Would any of you like to know what I believe God is doing among us?" Their response was unanimous, spontaneous, and over-whelming. "Yes! We want to know." It was then that I shared the Prayer Covenant. "I believe God is calling us to pray for each other daily and to ask Jesus to be the Lord of our lives for forty days." They said yes, and they did. I now had seventeen people for whom I was praying and who were praying daily for me that Jesus would be Lord of my life and guide me to be God's pastor for the College Hill Presbyterian congregation. Can you imagine the en-couragement and strength these people and their prayers gave me?

Because of this wonderful response, I decided to invite the congregation to enter into a Prayer Covenant with me. I was asking them to pray that Jesus would be Lord of their lives and that they would pray the same prayer for me. Hundreds of people entered into a Prayer Covenant with me and a spiritual revolution of Christ followers had begun! During this revolution there were some people who left the church, but there were many others who started coming.

God led wonderfully strong and capable leaders to join the staff. During these years the discovery and development of spiritual gifts became central to the life of the church. Members of the congregation were equipped, empowered and released to do ministry in and beyond the boundaries of College Hill Church.

Other Revolutions Begin

It was such a privilege and joy to work with so many staff and congregational members. We all experienced rich blessing as the ministry flowed out into Cincinnati and well beyond. While at College Hill, during this time of rich growth, I became increasingly concerned with the effect our increasingly sexualized culture was having on the church and on my church! The concern led to the founding of several ministries, including Citizens for Community Values, focused on Cincinnati, along with the Religious Alliance against Pornography and the National Coalition Against Pornography, the latter of which has since become a worldwide ministry called pureHope. I left the church in 1986 to found and lead the National Coalition Against Pornography but continued to be engaged for several years in the ongoing ministry at College Hill.

I had a strong sense of calling to start the coalition because I had seen and learned about what was happening to our young men and women. I learned from the FBI that one in seven young boys and one in three young women were being sexually molested before the age of eighteen. My heart was broken. I cried out to God, asking Him to do something about this crisis. I must admit that I was angry with God. His answer was, "I have done something about it and I am calling you to start this work!" I shared with my wife, Patty, that I believed that God was calling me to leave College Hill Church for at least a year to fight the battle against pornography. She thought I was foolish but was totally supportive. Sometimes, looking back on it, I think she might have been right.

Through the years I gathered a team of pastors and leaders who saw pornography as the root cause of sexual abuse and molestation and wanted to do something about it. The ministry eventually grew and had offices in Southern California, Kansas City, Atlanta, Charlotte, and New England. We met with two presidents and six attorneys general to strengthen law enforcement against illegal pornography. In partnership with the Religious Alliance against Pornography, we sponsored the first international conference focused on child pornography and child prostitution. The conference brought together more than 150 leaders from around the world and was held in Manila, Philippines. The host for the conference was the Roman Catholic cardinal of that region. His name was Cardinal Sin. God does have a sense of humor!

While leading the National Coalition Against Pornography, I was often accused of being against sex. My large family demonstrates that this was simply not true. God has blessed me with five children, twenty-eight grandchildren, and thirty-three great-grandchildren, with more on the way!

I left the ministry of pureHope after twenty-seven years, in 2013. I was retired for twenty-four hours before hearing God's call to begin the Prayer Covenant ministry. My sons, both of whom are pastors, encouraged me to explore a national ministry focused on encouraging and facilitating a Christ awakening undergirded by prayer.

What a delightful surprise the ministry of the Prayer Covenant has become! While we initially focused on adults in the United States, God has now moved the Prayer Covenant to over fifty countries, ministering primarily to children. In just the past four and a half years, the ministry has reached over 2.6 million children, with seventy thousand of them making a first-time commitment to Christ.

"Jesus, be Lord of my life" was the initial line of the Prayer Covenant, and while the prayer grew to include nine other lines, surrender to the Lordship of Christ remains central. The tagline for the Prayer Covenant ministry became "Following Jesus Together" and captures the importance of prayer in fellowship, accountability, and commitment to and with other believers. The mutual relational surrender to Jesus continues to be the heart of the Prayer Covenant ministry. A recent expression of this mutual surrender to Jesus is the Jesus Covenant Prayer Partners, a network of pastors and Christian leaders across the United States who pray, serve and share together in pursuit of a Christ awakening.

Growing in Spiritual Disciplines

A life principle that has guided me in every major decision is knowing, believing, praying, and living the Word of God. I have always practiced no Bible/no breakfast, no prayer/no paper. This discipline has served me well. I believe the Bible is the inspired Word of God. Memorizing verses and passages has been a joy, a source of great strength and a lifelong discipline. The call for all of God's people is to live out what the Scriptures teach through the presence and power of the Holy Spirit.

The Bible is the whole counsel of God, and there are many passages that have been vitally important to me. Two of these are John 7:38–39:

> Whoever believes in me, as the Scripture has said, rivers of living water will flow from within them. By this he meant the Spirit, whom those who believed in him were later to receive. Up to that time the Spirit had not been given, since Jesus had not yet been glorified...

And Ephesians 3:17–21:

> ...so that Christ may dwell in your hearts through faith. And I pray that you, being rooted and established in love, may have power, together with all the Lord's holy people, to grasp how wide and long and high and deep is the love of Christ, and to know this love that surpasses knowledge—that you may be filled to the measure of all the fullness of God. Now to him who is able to do immeasurably more

than all we ask or imagine, according to his power that is at work within us, to him be glory in the church and in Christ Jesus throughout all generations, for ever and ever! Amen.

For over sixty years of ministry I have seen God do more than I could ask or imagine. He has done so by using ordinary people like me and many others in extraordinary ways. To Him alone be all the glory.

6

Called to the Pulpit

Rich Lanning

I first met Rich when he joined the staff of Evangelical Community Church in 2004. Since 2005 he has been my senior pastor. I have had the privilege to sit under his wonderful teaching and preaching. Our relationship has grown very close over the years as I have served as a session member at the church. In this way we have worked together in leading the spiritual life of Evangelical Community Church members. God has blessed Evangelical Community Church in amazing ways under Rich's leadership. He has led us through a building campaign, a growing commitment to missions around the world and reaching out to our neighbors. Through his preaching, teaching, and leadership, Rich has challenged me to grow as a follower of Jesus.

In the past few years our relationship has gone to another level of fellowship and discipleship as I have served as his accountability partner. We meet every other month or so to talk about how we are doing as followers of our Lord Jesus. This has deepened my respect for Rich not only as my pastor but as a husband, father, and friend.

Rich's Story

I was born May 25, 1967, in Zanesville, Ohio, and moved to Cincinnati in 1969. My mom and dad were the greatest influence of my life. Jesus was always at the center of our home, and when we arrived in Cincinnati, we began attending Groesbeck Methodist Church. My mom taught third and fourth grade and shared the gospel regularly with the children she taught. I attended Central Baptist School through junior high then went to St. Xavier High School.

My faith journey was enriched when we began attending College Hill Presbyterian Church when I was in sixth grade. My mother, Linda, is a prayer warrior, and I am sure that she prayed for me regularly. She loved reading, studying, and sharing God's Word. My dad and mom were very active at College Hill and joined the evangelism team, led by Pastor Dr. Ron Rand. It seemed that my dad always had exciting stories every week when he came home from the evangelism teams' connections. I was always interested and excited to hear about the impact they were having on people's lives.

The staff at College Hill was very influential in my life as well as in the lives of my parents. I studied under Dr. Gary Sweeten, the discipleship pastor, and was inspired by his courses on practical Christian living. His courses, including Apples of Gold and Listening for Heaven's Sake, were especially helpful.

I smile to recall that my father, who was an assistant golf professional at Clovernook Country Club, taught well-known author and theologian Dr. R. C. Sproul to play golf. Because of this connection, I got my hands on many wonderful teaching tapes by R. C. They were profoundly formative in my love for theology, the church and the Scripture.

During this time, doors consistently opened for me to connect with ministry leaders, missionaries, and thoughtful Christians from around the world who were coming to be part of the powerful spiritual life of College Hill. My interaction with these individuals has continued to form my spiritual life. I was eager and ready when God spoke to me about going into full-time Christian ministry as a junior in high school.

The impact of these early years has given me a great desire to stand under (not just understand) the Word of God, to read good Christian books, and to seek out the teaching of some of God's great servants.

Key passages from the Bible for my life certainly include:

> Keep this Book of the Law always on your lips; meditate on it day and night.... Be strong and courageous. Do not be afraid; do not be discouraged, for the LORD your God will be with you wherever you go. (Josh. 1:8-9)

> But whose delight is in the law of the LORD,
>   who meditates on his law day and night.
> That person is like a tree ... Whatever they do
>   prospers. (Ps. 1:2-3)

Trust in the LORD with all your heart and lean
not on your own understanding;
in all your ways submit to him, and he will
make your paths straight. (Prov. 3:5-6)

Now to him who is able to do immeasurably
more than all we ask or imagine, according to
the power that is at work within us, to him be
glory in the church and in Christ Jesus
throughout all generations, for ever and ever!
Amen. (Eph. 3:20-21)

Transforming teachers have been R. C. Sproul, J. I.
Packer, Martin Lloyd Jones and the great Reformer John
Calvin. What a privilege it has been to read their books
and to learn from their insights and how they have lived
and served for the glory of God.

Early Years of Study and Ministry

I received an Evans scholarship, which was awarded to
aspiring young golf caddies based on their leadership, academic ability, community service, and need. This enabled
me to attend Miami University in Oxford, Ohio. While
there, I was very active in both InterVarsity and Campus
Crusade. During my senior year God confirmed His calling on my life to become a pastor. I graduated in 1989, and
Christy and I were married the following year.

I joined the summer staff at College Hill under the
leadership of Sybil Towner, who ran a children's and
youth ministry that affected people throughout Cincinnati. That was a wonderful life-shaping experience as she

mentored me. This tied my life even more deeply to College Hill and its outstanding, spiritually enriching ministry.

After that summer, I joined the staff at White Oak Presbyterian Church as the youth director under Pastor Bob Denny. I was deeply engaged in the entire church ministry, which gave me an even better perspective on a healthy church and how it functions. It, too, was a wonderful experience as Pastor Denny almost treated me as his pastoral assistant. I was even invited to preach on occasion. That inspired me with a passion for ministry and for proclaiming the Word of God. As the youth director, I led a Teen Breakfast Club for thirty-five to fifty kids weekly. I was privileged to lead youth mission trips and to disciple children, rooting them in the Word of God and challenging them to walk closely with Jesus. I smile with pleasure to mention that two of the members of that youth group, brothers Steve and Chris Doughman, are presently members with their families of my current congregation.

I left White Oak Presbyterian in fall 1993 to attend Gordon-Conwell Theological Seminary in the Boston area. My experience there was simply amazing. Three key elements of Gordon-Conwell's perspective shaped me dramatically: cultivating a mind for truth, developing a heart for God, and the presentation of the pastor/scholar model of ministry. My wife, Christy, and I entered into deep fellowship with other young couples. We had few financial resources, but we were excited to be on an adventure to serve the Lord together, so we shared a remarkable sense of community.

Among my outstanding professors were Haddon Robinson and Meredith Klein. Dr. Robinson taught homiletics—he inspired me to prepare and preach well. His respect for the Word of God grounded me in my preaching ministry. Dr. Klein was simply brilliant. He was a gifted teacher, scholar, and writer. He modeled what it means to love God and to pursue godly living in a scholarly manner. He was an ardent and effective defender of the faith. My affection and appreciation for Gordon-Conwell as a teaching institution has continued to deepen over the years as their commitment to serve and enrich, not compete with or replace the local church, has blessed me.

Serving the Church

After graduating from Gordon-Conwell, I was honored to return and serve for a year on the staff of White Oak Presbyterian. I then received a call from Calvin Church in Detroit and served there as Senior Pastor from 1998–2003. This was a brand-new experience for me, as I was the only pastor on staff. The church was situated in the heart of Detroit. We crossed racial and economic lines. Our members were hungry to be nurtured and discipled. I was challenged, affirmed, and encouraged in learning to do ministry in this urban context.

I joined the staff of Evangelical Community Church in Springdale, Ohio, in 2004 as the Interim Senior Pastor and then became the permanent pastor in 2005. The move to Evangelical Community Church began a time of personal fulfillment and the development and use of my gifts, which first began to show themselves when I was a young person at College Hill Presbyterian Church. My two greatest gifts are preaching and teaching. That is mildly ironic, as I am an introvert and enjoy being in the background and doing things behind the scenes.

As I function as a pastor in a suburban setting in the United States, I have been challenged to provide leadership for the church in a radically changing culture. The developing secularization of America has shifted and changed so many things about both America and the church. In many denominations there is a loss of spiritual vitality and Christian convictions. I am glad to say that in my congregation and in the Evangelical Presbyterian denomination, of which we are a part, this is not the case. Those who attend have an intentional Christian worldview, commitment to the Scriptures as the Word of God, and orthodox Christian values.

I have been active not only in teaching and preaching but in leadership of the staff and session. When we experience conflict, there has been a need for pastoral care. I find it fulfilling to address these issues and see members of our congregation grow in Christian maturity.

Evangelical Community Church's vision statement is "Following Jesus by Loving God, Loving One Another and Serving the World." This is our expression of both the Great Commandment and the Great Commission. We are deeply committed to making disciples. Our members are growing in confidence in their faith and in the Scriptures. Many of our adults and youth are studying God's Word regularly as part of our Christian discipleship ministry.

The church is active in world missions, church planting, and evangelizing the lost. Mission trips by our members to places such as Africa, Poland, and India both inspire and challenge us. We are regularly blessed to hear from our ministry partners and how God is using them to serve our great King Jesus. It is a privilege to pray for and support those who serve on our behalf.

Many of our members are active in leading, supporting and serving other ministries. These include the Coalition for Christian Outreach, Campus Crusade (now Cru), pro-life ministries, Matthew 25 Ministry, the Prayer Covenant, and many others. It is thrilling to see that Evangelical Community Church has a significant footprint in the Kingdom of God that is well beyond our size.

Our children and youth are being discipled by amazing teachers. They are growing in their walk with the Lord through our Sunday school ministry, mission trips, and service opportunities. Many are involved in our Sunday morning worship, and we are all blessed by them.

The Prayer Covenant and Evangelical Community Church

I have especially found the Prayer Covenant to be a powerful tool in my pastoral ministry. I knew of the Prayer Covenant because of my personal connection with Jerry Kirk, who was my pastor during the very influential College Hill years. The Prayer Covenant uses a thoughtful ten-line prayer that brilliantly touches on essential themes of biblical faith. Pastor Kirk encourages the use of the prayer in committed prayer partnerships.

Beginning several weeks before Lent, and for ten weeks total, I preached the Prayer Covenant line by line, finishing up just before Easter. I also invited both Jerry Kirk and Rick Schatz to share in the preaching series.

There were eighty people who made formal commitments to pray the prayer, although I believe there were more who used the prayer. Church members were encouraged not just to pray the prayer but also to enter into Prayer Covenant partnerships. They were encouraged not just to use the prayer cards but also to memorize the prayer.

I used the book *The Prayer Covenant* for sermon preparation and made it available for purchase by everyone in the congregation. Our community groups, which meet biweekly, used the book as the subject of their study as well.

I saw a number of benefits, and three stand out: First, the Prayer Covenant promoted prayer. There was a noticeable difference in the consciousness of prayer throughout the congregation. Prayer became intentional, not just something that was assumed. Not only were more people praying, but there was a sense of spiritual connection. I sensed the Lord was honoring our prayers.

Second, there was a discernable increase in spiritual vitality. The congregation seemed especially alive during the series. One leader of the church said that at the beginning of the series he was skeptical. When he started out, the prayer felt canned. However, shortly into the series, his attitude changed as the prayer came alive to him.

Third, the Prayer Covenant challenged me! At Jerry Kirk's encouragement, I prayed daily for every person who made a Prayer Covenant commitment, all eighty of them! Not only did this make prayer a primary part of my day, but it also created unexpected opportunities for pastoral care connections. For so many people in the church I was able to say, "I am praying for you. How is it going?"

Because of its significant impact, I have invited the congregation to enter into the Prayer Covenant with me several times since then. In every case more than 40 percent of our congregation has entered into the Prayer Covenant and I have continued to see growth in prayer and spiritual vitality every time we have done it.

God Is Growing Me and His Church at Evangelical Community Church

Family life is very important to me, although balancing my time between ministry and family needs remains a constant challenge. It is thrilling to see my wife and all six of my children committed to Christ and growing in their love for the Lord. I understand that my family is my legacy and that they are what I will leave behind when I go to meet my Savior. I don't see how any parent cannot be absolutely thrilled when there is great love and unity in their family and everyone is sold out for Jesus.

As a pastor, I have been blessed by seeing our church members grow in their confidence in the Scriptures and in what they believe. We are all growing together in our vision for the world, for discipleship and evangelism. Like the apostle Paul, we have certainly not arrived but we follow His example by "forgetting what is behind and straining toward what is ahead, I (we) press on toward the goal to win the prize for which God has called me (us) heavenward in Christ Jesus" (Philippians 3:13–14).

The saying is true: "God is good all the time. All the time God is good." I am blessed by His goodness as a pastor, husband, father, grandfather, and servant of our great God—Father, Son, and Holy Spirit.

7

Sexual Wholeness in Jesus

Jerry Armelli

Soon after I joined the staff of the National Coalition Against Pornography, the ministry began to address much more than just pornography. One of the cultural issues facing the church in the early nineties was that of same-sex attraction. The church had little to say on this issue except what was either harsh and judgmental or compromising of biblical truth. It seemed that Christians were unable to balance the need for truth and grace. Within the same-sex attracted community, the church had earned a reputation for being hateful and unloving or had embraced homosexuality as an acceptable lifestyle.

Since College Hill Presbyterian Church no longer had an effective ministry in this area, there was a void in greater Cincinnati of support and engagement for those who were same-sex attracted. That is when I learned about Exodus International and the ministry of Jerry Armelli. Exodus was able to bridge the gap between judgment and abdication of truth. Jerry headed the ministry for the Cincinnati area. I first met him in 1991 and was immediately impressed with his commitment to biblical truth on the issue and his caring and gentle spirit for those who were attempting to address unwanted same-sex attraction or *behavior in their lives. He was Jesus with skin on for this community. He had a genuine love for those who wanted to change and had a very real and personal understanding of the struggle.*

Jerry's approach was not to holler and scream "Sinner!" but to come alongside those who wanted to be free from unwanted sexual desires and behavior. His goal did not start with the idea of getting same-sex attracted people to become heterosexuals. His starting place for every believer in Jesus, including those with unwanted same-sex attraction, was the development of the desire to be holy, to follow Jesus in every area of their lives. There was no compromise of biblical truth in Jerry's approach. He knew that the Scriptures saw all sexuality outside the marriage of one man to one woman as falling short of God's desire for His people.

As I have gotten to hear more of Jerry's message and to see his ministry in action, I have seen the Lord bless his approach and his personal life as well. He is serving others with the love of Christ, and God is producing significant fruit from Prodigal Ministries, which he leads. His personal journey is a powerful testimony of our extraordinary God working through one of His ordinary people. I pray that you will be encouraged by it.

Jerry's Story

Aesop's fable "The Fox and the Grapes" is the perfect parable about my early life and gender-identity development. In the fable, a very hungry fox tries over and over again to pluck grapes that hang temptingly from a vine overhead. He jumps and he jumps, but he cannot reach them. He finally gives up and says in disgust, "Aw, they're probably sour grapes anyway. Who wants sour grapes? They're not worth it."

That was me exactly, with the male world around me. To me, the grapes in this story represent male bonding, acceptance, and inclusion. They represent the masculine affirmation that I craved desperately but could never seem to obtain. I wanted to be one of the guys, to belong, to have their qualities, their characteristics, and their physique. Admiration turned to envy, and I coveted what I perceived they had but I didn't: masculinity.

When I couldn't get from them what I legitimately pined for, I became angry and resentful. I said, "Aw, they're stupid boys anyway. They have stupid games. They're cut off from themselves. All they know about is sports—how shallow. They don't want relationships. They're just a bunch of idiots. I hate them." The grapes of masculinity, I told myself, were sour anyway. I rejected them even as I craved them. Both feelings, in direct opposition to each other, were intensely strong. Talk about confusing!

I got involved in theater and dance. These activities kept me safe from the feelings of not belonging in the "real masculine world." My father, brothers, and peers didn't know how to relate to me. So again, I knew I was different from other boys. I was teased and mocked for different things about me—the way I walked, talked, laughed, or for the things I did. I would often receive contemptuous looks from boys that said I was a disgrace. I saw those looks and thought they were telling me, "You're an embarrassment to all males." I felt I just didn't measure up. What I was made of was not acceptable to males. I concluded that real males have bigger bodies and participate in things such as football, wrestling, and fighting, and I don't. Something must be wrong with me. But what is it?

What's wrong with me that they don't like me and I can't be like them? When they wouldn't accept me, I rejected them in order to protect myself. "The grapes are sour anyway."

Instead of meeting these challenges head-on and fighting for my place in the circle of men, I tended to avoid whatever activity or challenge caused that feeling of inadequacy, of being different, of being less than other men. I would try to avoid activities associated with the masculine realm. I needed a nurturing, benevolent male to coach me, but none ever came forward.

Seeking Answers

Immediately, I set out on two quests. The first was to find out whether I was really homosexual or just going through a phase. I thought, first of all, I'd better find out what's going on within me, before I do something that I'm going to regret for the rest of my life. I found a psychologist, a Jewish woman, and I just talked. I was basically coming out to myself. I would talk, and in that whole process, the conclusion seemed to be obvious: "I'm homosexual." She didn't pronounce me a homosexual. I came to that conclusion myself as I told another person for the first time in my life about my long sexual relationship with this older guy and my feelings about it.

I resigned myself that I wasn't just confused but I really was a homosexual. It was very grievous, to think that I would never marry or have children.

Having labeled myself as homosexual, I set about on my second quest, which was to find out what God wanted me to do about it. I said, "God, if you say it's OK to go into the 'gay,' I will. If not, I won't." Simple as that. Black or white.

I had been raised Roman Catholic. I went to Catholic schools and a Catholic college. My parents raised me with excellent morals and values that I had internalized and that were important to me. I had to know that the life path I would choose was acceptable to God.

I came out to one of my friends who was gay, and he took me to my first gay bar and my first gay party. It was scary but exciting. I started dating men. I visited gay organizations and participated in their activities, all the while continuing my quest to find out what God wanted me to do with my homosexuality. I was on a spiritual quest as much as a sexual, emotional, or social one. Any questions I had in my mind, I wanted to face them, right then and there, before I got sexually involved with anyone.

I would say to myself, *So many things are wrong here. Could it really be okay with God?* These things were glaring things to me. I felt like when I went in, I was handed this pretty little present in a box that said, "Everything is taken care of for you. You just talk this way. You just do these things. You go to these places. You sleep with these men." I was rather bold, because I wouldn't accept the package the gay community offered me. I thought, *If this is so right, if you believe this is so true, if this is so valid, then why can't we discuss this honestly and thoroughly?*

To my advantage, I didn't deny these things, and I appreciated my parents for the morals and values they instilled in me. I didn't sleep with anybody through this whole process—which made me an oddity even in the gay community. In fact, I was told by a gay man, "Quit coming around here if you're not going to 'put out.'" Despite the years of the closeted sexual relationship I had in my adolescence, I had decided I was not going to sleep with another guy until we were in love or we made a permanent commitment to each other, like a marriage. They just couldn't understand it.

I think because I was celibate through this time, my sexual desires didn't get tangled up with my spiritual quest and confuse my heart and mind. I was able to see the gay subculture more clearly for what it really was. And I didn't like what I saw.

Next, I sought answers from Dignity, the pro-gay Catholic group that affirms men and women in being gay. But I found Dignity's message was not about purity, nor about celibacy, nor about faith, nor about relationship with God. It wasn't even about Catholicism. It just seemed like a gay bar, only without the alcohol, to me. It was terrible. I felt worse after going there than I did at the gay bar.

Seeking answers from other people was equally confusing. Some straight people were telling me, "It's okay to 'go gay.' It's no big thing." Other people were saying, "It's wrong. I don't understand it, but it's wrong." As for religious people, likewise, some were saying it's okay, some were saying it's not. Psychologists were saying it's okay, just be true to yourself. And of course, gays were telling me it's okay. But something within me was telling me it was not good, and I still hadn't found my answer from God.

I fell into a deep depression. I thought, *I'm homosexual, and is going "gay" all there is? I don't want that kind of a life! It's not for me. There's no life in it.* I wanted to reverse time—like I had never come out—but I couldn't. It was out now, and I could never go back into the closet. I felt hopeless. I thought, *No matter what I do, I'll never be happy.* And then the thoughts started coming into my head: *Just take your life. If you go back inside yourself, you're going to be unhappy, or if you go "gay," you'll never be happy. Just take your life.*

I remember standing in the shower one time, heavy with depression. I literally felt myself starting to collapse. I sensed I was about to have a psychotic breakdown. But all of a sudden, I felt these large, supernatural, spiritual hands behind my back lifting me back up on my feet. I felt a surge of strength, and small voice whispered, "Keep going." I recognized immediately that it was the Lord intervening, giving me His strength to lean on when I couldn't do it by myself any longer.

Movement Toward Safety

In the theater realm, I was comfortable and safe. There were no jocks there, and people were sensitive and interested in relationships. They affirmed my gifts and talents instead of rejecting them.

The further and further I moved away from males to avoid these feelings of inadequacy and avoid the rejection, the more I gravitated toward females. Girls were safe and nonthreatening. They didn't expect me to be big and aggressive. In fact, they liked me to be social and sensitive. Girls liked me to play house with them so I could play the father. Being with girls didn't dredge up all the feelings of inadequacy and fear and intimidation. It was very safe.

The more time I spent with my girl buddies in those critical developmental years, the more I began identifying and acting like them. I became increasingly effeminate. That of course only made me more different from boys and caused them to reject me all the more. I was called sissy, fag, and queer. As the chasm separating me from males got bigger and bigger, the more I rejected them. Now they were hurting me more directly.

I became angrier. No longer trying to fit in, I used this effeminacy to rebel against my adversary—my male peers. I used it as a weapon to mock their masculinity and to try to make them feel uncomfortable. I used it to push them further away and tried to hurt them, as I perceived they were hurting me.

Growing up, I felt so different from other males that they actually started to appear to be the opposite gender from me. Men were unknown to me. A mystery. I wondered, *Who are they? What are they about? I don't understand them. What do they feel like?* This sense of mystery, fascination, and wonder is what males typically experience about females, especially during adolescence and young adulthood, and females for males, which drives much of their sexual interest in each other. Opposites attract. But I was so disengaged from my male peers that I was experiencing this sense of mystery with them rather than with girls. This started well before puberty. Once I entered puberty, these feelings easily turned erotic.

At the age of eleven, a boy whose masculinity I admired and was intimidated by sexually molested me. He was part of the group of boys I admired and hated. I admired him because he had the physique, he had the sports trophies, he had the status, and he had the male friends that I didn't have. I really wanted to be friends with him the same way the other boys were friends with each other, but we never had that kind of real relationship.

After high school, I joined a dance company and trained to become a professional ballet dancer. Ironically, this was tremendously affirming to my masculinity because of the rigorous physical workout of dance and the clearly defined roles of men and women in the dance. To display masculine strength and male-female dynamics through dance was very empowering and affirming.

When I was twenty-three, I was in a show, and another man in the show was giving me a lot of attention. I found myself becoming excited by it. Then a friend of his came up to me and said, "Jerry, Joe is gay and he likes you. Are you gay?" And I remember a long pause, and I remember saying, "I don't know."

I don't know! For the first time I let the idea come out of my unconscious that I might be homosexual. Believe it or not, in all my confusion and throughout my long adolescent sexual relationship with another guy, I never consciously labeled myself as homosexual. I knew I was different, but I hadn't labeled myself "gay." Now, asked point blank, I didn't have an answer.

The Journey to Real Answers

So I hung on and continued my search. I talked with the chaplain at my former high school, and he invited me to a charismatic Catholic prayer group. I said, "Yes, I'll try anything." When I walked past the foyer of the church and entered the doors of the main sanctuary, I felt a little voice speaking as if from inside of me that said, "You're home. The war is over, and you're finally home." It was like nails that had been sticking in my back, holding me down for so long, had suddenly been released as I stepped foot into the sanctuary.

It was in that group that I met Jesus as real, living, active, involved, and personal. Over the next few weeks, I recognized Jesus as my Savior. I didn't invite Him into my life to save me from homosexuality specifically. Rather, I knew that I was a sinner and that I needed Him to atone for my sins, and I wanted His strength, guidance, and love with me always. I gradually made Him the Lord of my life—and my life began to transform. I decided to follow the principles and the directives of the Bible, which are so life changing!

The love in that prayer circle was tangible. During one particularly powerful prayer, I heard the words, from inside of me, speak softly but with conviction: "Homosexuality is wrong, Jerry. To act on it is wrong. The behavior is wrong, and the condition is not what I have for you. Follow me, Jerry, in a close relationship, and I will change your life." And I said, "Lord, I will make you shepherd of my life. You are the first man I have ever trusted enough not to hurt me. So I'm going to let you love me."

What tremendous healing that brought my wounded heart. Finally, I invited a masculine love source into my heart, and it was the true masculine, the divine masculine, not the broken machismo of a broken generation. Finally, I had a true man to model myself after and one to affirm me in my unique masculinity.

With my heart opened to masculine love and a new sense of courage in facing relationships with those I once saw as my adversaries—other males—I learned to forgive.

I came to forgive those who I felt had sinned against me and to be forgiven for those I sinned against through my contempt and bitterness. I committed myself to be obedient to God, no matter what my feelings said. My new faith taught me to get outside of myself and build healthy relationships with men, women, and family.

I pursued my dreams and goals and stopped focusing all of my life on this one aspect of my life, my sexuality. I found tremendous healing. My thoughts and feelings about myself and my identity started to change.

At one point, I pondered the story of Abraham and Isaac, and the fact that Abraham was willing to sacrifice his own son out of obedience. I realized I should be willing to go that far, to sacrifice my sexuality and romantic relationships, if God asked it. The thought of never loving someone, either a man or a woman, as fully as I desired hurt me deeply. I wept. But I determined to do as Abraham did and sacrifice my greatest desire. And as He did with Abraham, God intervened and honored my willingness to sacrifice. He knew the intent of my heart. In response, He filled my life with joy. Replacing my years of turmoil and grief and sorrow, He brought joy into my life and into my heart.

The joy I felt in my relationship with Jesus became a platform to then say, "You know, if He loves me and accepts me, then I have no reason to be afraid of another man, or feel intimidated by men." So I could begin to take risks and be in relationship with other men. Finally, I could let other men into my heart. Before, I had kept them out because they were hurtful, but I began to say, "They can't hurt me because my relationship with Jesus has taken the power away from them. They don't hold the keys to my life. I don't need them to approve of me for me to be okay."

One difficult hurdle in this regard was overcoming my craving and validation from men, particularly my brothers. When I was accepted into my first professional ballet company and got the lead, I thought to myself, *Finally my brothers will see how accomplished and athletic I am as a dancer. Sure, I don't have the sports trophies that they have, but what I have accomplished is better. I am a professional dancer, a professional athlete. They will affirm me just like they were affirmed about their accomplishments.*

But my brothers didn't respond the way I wanted them to respond. In fact, they said and did nothing! I was heartbroken. I was hurt and angry. But as I prayed, a peace came over me as I realized, "Jerry, you want your brothers' approval, but you don't need it. Christ has given you all the approval you need, and His affirmation is the one you need the most."

From that day on, I learned I could move among men knowing I was as capable and as adequate as them, unique yet equal too! I began to discover that I really was like them and they really were like me. My sense of alienation from men began to fall away. I stopped seeing the grapes as sour or out of reach. I was becoming free.

Soon I met some new Christian friends who discipled me. One in particular, a married man named Michael who was also a dancer, took me under his wing as a man to a man. He loved me unconditionally. He mentored me as a man and as a Christian. I began to feel my needs for healthy male companionship and identity being met. Despite all the baggage of my history, despite my dependency and lingering effeminacy, he stayed in a healthy relationship with me. I found myself growing in manhood and masculinity.

During that time, I was baptized. I felt at home and encouraged to grow further into heterosexuality. When I got up to be baptized, I stood at the microphone and said boldly, "Satan tried to lie me into homosexuality, but I called upon Jesus, and He saved me." The people rose up in a standing ovation. It was tremendously powerful. The word was coming out. I was not hiding any more. I was not ashamed of my past, and I wanted to share the message that no one need be. There is no shame in coming out of homosexuality—it should be cheered!

Those five years were blissfully healing. Michael helped me understand, and the Spirit confirmed, that I was to reflect the unique masculinity that God created me to express, a facet of masculinity that God had uniquely given to me. I wasn't to pursue anyone else's or covet anyone else's masculinity, and no one could shame mine because God had given it to me to reflect Him.

Later I moved in with two roommates who knew my past, but it wasn't an issue to them. I was just one of the guys! Finally, I was in a place emotionally where I could relate to them as a man equal to them.

As I shared my story with others, someone said to me, "Have you met Bob? Have you met Joseph? They came out of homosexuality too."

I said, "Oh my gosh, there are others who came out of homosexuality?" Soon we met and shared our stories. We felt God wanted us to do more with our experience. We knew that there were and are hundreds and thousands of men and women out there who believe there is no hope for change, who are going down a road to death, who are living hopelessly depressed lives. What did God want us to do about it?

The Ministry Begins

The answer came: open a phone line and start a support group. We did that in 1986. I obtained my Bachelor's degree and went on to graduate school and got my Master's in Counseling. I was then hired at a local professional counseling agency, where I was mentored and felt very affirmed by the Director. I later moved on to work full time at Prodigal Ministries.

At Prodigal Ministries, I made a new friend, a musician who invited me to choreograph and dance in a piece he was writing called "The Atonement." I was honored to do so. My dance partner would be his sister, Mia, who was also a professional dancer.

I soon found myself interested in Mia in ways I never had been interested in a woman before. We started dating, but she warned me that she was not interested in a relationship because she had just come out of a five-year relationship with a man that had ended badly. That was fine with me. I was more than happy to take it slow and become friends first, then cautiously explore romance with her later. Two years after our first date, I asked her to marry me. We were married six months later. Today we have a beautiful daughter together.

I am at the point in my life now where homosexuality is no longer a struggle. I had to go through a lot of barricades—psychologically, spiritually, and emotionally. I am now very fulfilled in my life. Today I identify with other heterosexual men as my peers, my brothers, and my equals. I am in love with my wife. I love being a husband and a daddy. And most of all, I love my heavenly Father, who reached out and showed this prodigal son the way home, and then welcomed him with open arms.

8

Reaching the Unreached: Part 1

Peter

Diane and Peter train and disciple ambassa-
dors who are reaching the Muslim world for the Prince of Peace.
Their work is not only challenging but has had its risks as well,
as they lived in the Middle East for more than twenty-five years.
Their love for the Muslim people should challenge each of us. We
are called to see Muslims as persons who are the object of God's
love. Jesus came to seek and save the lost, and this includes those
who are of the Muslim faith.

In order to include their story but not compromise their
safety, we are not using real names or specific places and times.
Because of this need for confidentiality and safety, my
introductory comments will be brief. I have known Peter and
Diane for many years. They have heard the call of God to go to
those with little or no Christian witness and have gone as an act
of obedience. It has been a privilege to partner with them
through prayer and support. They have been used powerfully by
God in sharing the gospel with many who had never before
heard of the real Jesus or met a Christian. They have been

blessed through God's calling but have been greatly challenged as well.

This couple has shared the gospel directly in the work of evangelism and has also served God in strengthening ministry teams. They have been used to increase the effectiveness of others through mentoring and discipleship. I wish I could be specific about this part of their work, but that would compromise their safety and identity.

Peter's Story

The Formative Impact of Other People on My Life

In the summer before university, the youth pastor of the church I attended invested time in me, prayed for me and taught me basic biblical principles. When I went to a different city to begin college, I sought out contact with a man on staff with a campus ministry. He continued my discipleship and taught me how to share the good news of Jesus with other students. We and the other students involved in the ministry met weekly in a large group and during the week in small discipleship groups. We strategized how we could share the gospel with every student in the dormitories. Eventually I was asked to be the male leader of the student side of that ministry.

Friends from our campus ministry and I attended a church away from the school so that we would have more exposure to Christians of all ages, not just college students. I was deeply influenced by the gifting, teaching, and examples of the pastoral staff of that church, and by the faithfulness of mature, wholesome Christian families who were in leadership.

I grew up in a churchgoing family. In elementary school, I was actively involved in Sunday school and earned the God and Country award in Boy Scouts. However, by the time I reached high school age, my parents stopped going to church and so did I. At first, I felt uneasy about not going to church, but I eventually got over that feeling. On the other hand, I had a very sensitive conscience about right and wrong, which stayed with me even as I entered mid-teenage years.

My parents moved the summer before my final year of high school. This meant I had to enter my senior year not knowing anyone in a class where friendships and cliques were already firmly established. This could have been an especially difficult time for a teenager like me, but God sovereignly used it to change my life forever.

Some of my classmates invited me to evening meetings where they learned about the Bible. At first, I declined, but then I noticed that these students had three things in common: they were intelligent, they were fun-loving, and they loved Jesus. Up to that point, I didn't know that combination was possible. After a few months of meetings, the leader clearly explained to me why Jesus came to earth and died on the cross. I wanted my guilty conscience to be cleansed, so I received the forgiveness of Jesus. In my heart and mind, I felt the experience of becoming a new creation in Christ. The old passed away, and the new came (2 Corinthians 5:17–20). Along with other students, I started attending a church recommended by the man who led me to Christ. I studied the Bible, read Christian books and shared Jesus with classmates.

My parents divorced two months before my high school graduation. To me this was a surprise but not a shock. Our household had been full of tension and strife for as long as I remembered. As I look back at the timing of their divorce, I am thankful that God had already planted me into a new spiritual family of Christians and I had begun to grow roots.

The Calling of God on My Life

I entered university planning to become a lawyer. However, by my second year I had been so involved in ministry on campus that I began to reconsider my career path. God brought three significant influences in my life that set me on my life's course. The first influence was Bible passages such as Matthew 28:18–20, which calls Christians to go into all the world to make disciples. I had already been making disciples on my college campus, but I newly understood the implications of the phrase "all the world."

The second influence God used was statistics—who would have thought!? I learned the demographics of where the gospel had spread in the world, which people groups had access to the gospel and spiritually speaking which were the neediest places on earth. The third influence was reading biographies of missionaries. I was inspired and challenged by the faith, perseverance and courage of pioneers who dedicated their lives to bring the love of Jesus to people who had no other human way of hearing about Him.

Rather than ask myself, *Why should I go to the unreached?* I asked, *What is keeping me from going?* I looked at my life. At that time, Luke 12:48 spoke to my deep heart: "From everyone who has been given much, much will be demanded." I had been given physical health, a good mind, a university education, and solid biblical disciple-ship. I had no financial or family obligations that would hold me back. I had been given much and much would be required of me. I decided to invest all I had been given for ministry to the unreached. Like Isaiah, I said to the Lord, "Here I am. Send me!" (Isa. 6:8).

While I was discerning God's call on my life, He gave me a gift of immeasurable value in a young woman of like mind and heart. Diane and I had much in common. We had both come to personal faith in Jesus less than a year before university. Both of us were the only evangelical Christians in our families. We were both from middle-class backgrounds and attended a public university. When we became the respective male and female leaders of our student campus ministry, we prayed together regularly.

We married soon after we graduated from university and together decided to ask God where He wanted us to serve. After a few years, God directed us to be His ambas-sadors among Muslims in the Middle East.

From One Calling to Multiple Callings

With my marriage to Diane, God gave me two more call-ings: to be a godly husband and (eventually) father. I am sorry to stay that it took me some years to understand that those two new callings were just as spiritual— even more so—than my call to be an ambassador for Christ to the na-tions. In the years to come, prioritizing and balancing those three calls was a huge challenge for me.

During one of our early years in the Middle East, a dear couple from our home church named Lou and Eileen visited with us for a week or so. I took Lou to visit some of my Muslim friends. Lou and Eileen listened as I explained all my heavy responsibilities sharing the gospel of Jesus with Muslims, leading a team of other cross-cultural workers, heading a family of two little children, and so on. They stayed in our apartment with us, and they observed firsthand my attitudes, words, and actions regarding my ministry and my family.

Toward the end of their visit, Lou said just a few firm but gentle words to me that lit a candle of light in my heart. He said, "Peter, you only get one chance in life as a husband and father. God can call lots of other people to share Jesus with Muslims here. But at the end of your life when you face the Lord, you are the only man He will ask, 'How well did you care for Diane and these precious children I gave you?'" I am thankful that Lou was wise, caring, and courageous enough to show me I had my priorities and attitudes out of proportion. His words jump-started me on a growing process that has continued the rest of my life.

In the next few years, we added new team members who needed our care and training in ministry. Our relationships with Muslims increased in numbers and depth. We began discipling and gathering new believers in Jesus. My calling as an ambassador to Muslims was in high gear.

Our pioneer work among Muslims was growing to the point that I invited a ministry consultant named Richard to fly from the States to help us think through how to organize new believers in Jesus from a Muslim background into house churches. I took him to visit my team members and local new believers in Jesus. Richard stayed in our home with us, just like Lou and Eileen had.

One day I decided to be vulnerable with Richard. I admitted that though I was extremely busy, I didn't feel like I was accomplishing all I could in my personal relationship with God, my ministry, and my family. I had half hoped that Richard would say something others had already said to me, like, "C'mon, Peter, don't be so hard on yourself. You're working day and night in a strategic ministry. Lighten up."

However, Richard said this: "Peter, from what I've seen and what you have said, I think that you have a besetting sin of passivity. Now, the word 'passive' is not in the Bible, but James 4:17 sums it up: 'If anyone, then, knows the good they ought to do and doesn't do it, it is sin for them.'"

Richard's words felt like a hammer to my forehead — not because they were wrong, but because they were right. Though I had been working hard for my ministry, I had been passive in developing my relationships with God, my wife, and my children. Richard's words fanned the candle flame that Lou had shone in my heart a few years earlier into a refining fire.

The Holy Spirit immediately granted me the gift of repentance. I repented to the Lord and sought Diane's forgiveness for making my ministry a higher priority than her and the kids. Over the next few years, with God's grace and Diane's patience, I reordered the priorities of my heart to reflect all of God's callings in my life: child of God, husband, father, and ambassador for Christ. I learned that these callings do not conflict with one another, nor do they take an equal amount of time or energy to fulfill. The main point was that I began correctly ordering them in my mind, heart, and calendar.

Twenty-five years later, I have more strategic opportunities and significant ministry invitations than I can possibly fulfill. I am still learning to answer requests by saying, "I'm sorry, but I have to decline your invitation." It's hard for me to turn down opportunities, but I believe it is easier after more than two decades of practice putting ministry in right perspective with my other spiritual callings as husband and father.

Challenges and Disappointments

After about a decade of living among Muslims in the Middle East, God gave me multiple opportunities for mutually respectful interfaith dialogues with influential leaders of a persecuted minority Muslim group of several million. This group's faith and culture are a unique blend of Islam, mysticism, and humanism, along with some values that overlap with the teachings of Jesus and the New Testament.

From this group's perspective, we had significant values in common: love of God, love of people, an aversion to religious legalism and hypocrisy, and a desire for religious tolerance in society. They and we had also experienced various degrees of misunderstanding, prejudice, and intolerance from the Muslim majority group.

Over a period of over ten years, I was invited by leaders of this group to contribute to several of their publications and speak at various events. My writing and speaking focused on our common faith values, especially ones that contrasted with those of the Muslim majority group. They loved Jesus' interactions with the Pharisees, whom they compared to the legalistic and hypocritical

Muslims who persecuted them. They wanted to know more about the biblical Jesus, so I explained Jesus' teachings and other Bible passages where our values came from. Very few of this group has ever seen or touched a real Bible.

Of course, my hope and prayer in those years was that God's promise in Isaiah 55:11 would come true: "My word that goes out from my mouth ... will not return to me empty, but will accomplish what I desire." God had opened unique doors for me to present His word to those who had not heard it and who, on the surface, were receptive to hearing it. I believed that His purpose was for these dear people to be reconciled to Him and become new creatures in Jesus (2 Cor. 5:17–20). I was further encouraged that, of the relatively small number of people in their country who followed Jesus, a significant proportion was from this group. So when I was invited by them to reveal in their magazines and on their radio programs that some of their most strongly held values are in the Bible, I expected the living and active Word of God to speak powerfully to their hearts (Heb. 4:11).

I believed my message was getting through when an educated and intelligent member of this group read one of my articles and said to me, "Peter, when our people read this, they are going to think that our historical religious leaders took all these teachings from Jesus and never told us where they got them!"

"Really?" I responded, smiling inside. I prayed silently, "Yes, Lord, open their minds to understand the Scriptures."

Then, in just a few months' time, the leaders I had been dialoguing with all moved to different locations or positions. Others who did not know me took their places. Invitations for me to write and speak dried up. The door was closed. To this day, I have no visible evidence that any seeds I sowed in those dozen years germinated and bore lasting fruit among this group.

Am I disappointed or discouraged? It is true that I wonder why God hasn't shown me visible fruit from those years of hard work, thought, and prayer, when the time and climate seemed so right. And I wonder why faithful, mature, and competent colleagues of mine who are still investing their lives as ambassadors to this group don't see much fruit either.

As I ponder those questions, God has reminded me again of the lesson I learned more than forty years ago when I was a new Christian sharing my faith with mixed results in the dormitories, fraternities, and classrooms of my university. I am called to live a godly life and per-suade others of the biblical Jesus (2 Cor. 5:11). Whether, when, or how the sovereign Lord chooses to use my tes-timony and witness is up to Him. It's all about God work-ing in the hearts of people who hear His word. It's not about the messenger.

God's sovereignty was clearly apparent in other ways during those years I spent dialoguing with that Muslim minority group. During a time when Muslim fundamen-talist emotions and violent persecutions where height-ened, a so-called journalist looking for a sensational story displayed my photo on national television and made slanderous accusations about my relationship with the minority group. He then provoked the police to come to my office to investigate me "to see if my papers were in order."

Like any good husband and father, my first concern was the safety and security of my wife and children, but I had no legal grounds to ask for protection. All I could do was pray with Diane, remind both of us that we were in the Lord's sovereign hands and hope that none of our friends, our neighbors, or men of ill intent saw the TV program.

If any of our friends or neighbors saw the slanderous TV program, they never mentioned it. We received no verbal or physical threats from anyone.

However, less than a year later, the same so-called journalist accused me in a national newspaper of being a spy posing as a religious worker attempting to create division in the country. He also identified the neighborhood where my office was located. When a local pastor friend of mine read the article he said, "Peter, this guy is pointing you out as a target."

We trusted God's sovereignty again, but we still needed to ask important questions. Should I stay away from my office for a while? (Yes.) Should I move my office? (No.)

The sovereign Lord chose to let us weather that storm without external harm. We faced no similar tests for the rest of our years in the Middle East.

More to do with the health of my soul than our physical safety, I also had to ask myself these questions: How can I forgive this man for the stress he has given us and the danger he has exposed us to—twice? And how will I know when I have forgiven him completely?

I prayed a prayer of intent to forgive him, knowing that the process of full forgiveness might take some time.

About six years later, God sovereignly gave me an opportunity to see that my forgiveness process was indeed complete. One day while I was getting a haircut, the barber turned the shop's TV to a program hosted by — guess who? I hadn't seen or heard of this so-called journalist since his last exposé of me.

As I watched this man's arrogance and self-importance emanate from the screen, I was assured in my heart that I had completely forgiven him. How did I know? Because acid did not spurt into my stomach at the sight of him, and I spontaneously prayed for his soul out of true concern rather than anger. I smiled and thanked the Lord for this providential gift.

Blessings, Joys, Legacy

As I look back now with perspective on these years of ministry, I am grateful to God for so many things. I smile warmly when I think of the ways that God has worked through me and my family for the advancement of His Kingdom.

A few of the blessings that come to mind include:

- The privilege of introducing the gospel of Jesus in their own language to hundreds of Muslims who had never met an evangelical Christian or seen a Bible

- Personal relationships with national believers continuing after more than twenty-five years

- Deep personal relationships of twenty to thirty years with coworker families from a number of countries

- Being used by God to bring peace and reconciliation between Christian leaders who have offended each other in the course of their ministries

- Being used by God to train and oversee field leaders in cross-cultural ministry and hear testimonies such as, "If it weren't for you and Diane, we would have given up and gone home"

- Seeing our ministry materials published, adopted, and used by a number of churches and ministries around the world

- I feel humbled that our sovereign Father has used an ordinary couple from non-evangelical American Midwestern families to be invited to more than twenty countries to train and mentor cross-cultural workers in biblical ministry skills.

9

Reaching the Unreached:
Part 2

Diane

Diane's Story

My childhood was typical for the time period that I grew up in—the late fifties and sixties in southwest Ohio. My family was loving and stable and I experienced a normal childhood with the exception that we didn't go to church. I first went to church at the invitation of a friend of mine in the fourth grade and wanted to keep going. I continued to attend this church and my parents took me so I could participate in youth group and sing in the choir. My mother attended from time to time. I enjoyed going, but there wasn't an emphasis on a personal walk with Jesus, which later became the center of my life. It wasn't until after I graduated from high school that I gave my life to the Lord at an all-church event in our town. I heard of the Lord's personal love for me and my need to decide to follow Him. I stood up and gave my life to Jesus—I had no idea what all that meant, but I was soon to find out!

When I entered university, the Lord gave me a gift that only now I can fully grasp how wonderful it was—I was paired with a roommate who loved the Lord. Elaine and I became fast friends, and together we attended a college ministry on our campus. There weren't many who attended given that it was such a large campus, but the friends I made there are still among those I dearly treasure to this day.

In my college years, as my faith was stretched and challenged, I realized that I wasn't drawn to a career in design, which I had chosen before I came to faith. I took a required anthropology course that was taught by a woman who blatantly claimed that God did not exist. I clearly remember a question on the final exam—"God is made in man's image," true or false. It was a moment of testing, and I deliberately chose the truthful answer that I knew would be marked as wrong. Faith to me was more important than a grade at that point. Later life's tests had greater consequences.

My Life Mate

I met Peter there in our freshman year. He attended the same campus ministry, and our lives intersected weekly. In our third year we both stepped into leadership roles in the ministry, and we spent more time together as our love grew. We were married right after we graduated.

We spent a year as interns at our church preparing for ministry in China. Then we worked with an organization that focused on mobilizing Christians to pray and go to

the people groups in the world who had the least opportunity to hear about Jesus. This was our introduction to a
community of likeminded people who were passionate
about seeing the unreached peoples of the earth reached
with the love of Jesus. We worked among gifted people,
some preparing to go to the field and many who had lived
on the field for years. In the course of our six years' preparation, China opened its communication with the world,
and it became apparent there were millions more Chinese
Christians than had previously been thought. We wanted
to go somewhere with greater need for the gospel. So we
set our sights on a virtually 100 percent Muslim country in
the Middle East.

The Move to the Middle East

With our two-year-old son, John, and when I was five
months pregnant, we moved to the Middle East as ambas-
sadors for Jesus. We never used the word "missionary,"
for in a Muslim's mind that meant that a person was paid
by a foreign government to convert people to be Christians with the enticements of money, foreign women, and
alcohol. We told our new acquaintances that we loved
God and He led us to live in their country. That introduction either opened up conversations or closed them, once
we had enough local language to be able to talk with our
neighbors and others we met.

Those early years overseas were filled with stress.
Learning a new language and culture was a full-time job,
but we also had a myriad of other responsibilities as
workers, and just to live there took a lot of time. Shopping
was especially an adventure with two little kids, John and

Hope, in a stroller on dilapidated sidewalks and roads. Large supermarkets didn't come to our country until the mid-1990s, so when we shopped, we went to many little shops to buy bread, meat, fruits and vegetables, and so on. Water and electricity outages were the norm in those days.

We learned to adapt and found a rhythm for living. We made good friends and we had fellowship with our teammates. We grew to love living there even with the ministry side of life being formidable. Our faith was constantly challenged or attacked—Muslims claimed we Christians believed in three gods, that Jesus didn't die on the cross, and that the Bible has been changed and corrupted so as not to be reliable as God's Word. In their minds it was unthinkable for a Muslim to become a Christian. They would say, "To be a citizen of our country equals being a Muslim." We referred to ourselves as followers of Jesus because the word "Christian" carries so much historical baggage that it didn't convey what we wanted to talk about—a loving relationship of our lives yielded to the Lordship of Jesus the Savior.

Peter spent much of his time meeting Muslim men and teaching English at a language school. We often had locals over for dinner in the evenings, which meant at least one or two full days of cooking for me to fix a meal with all the courses that they expected. In the early years I had to learn a great deal about what was required of me. I tried hard to meet those standards, but my heart struggled with expectations that weren't clear, especially when we weren't finding Muslims interested in knowing the Lord. I served countless little tulip-shaped glasses of tea over the course of two-plus decades and found my heart struggling with God's call on our lives in a seemingly very unfruitful place. What was the Lord asking of us?

My time outside our apartment was limited with young children in tow. We were very close to our neighbors, a family with three teenagers. Conversations were often centered on cooking and family. I made it a point to not become entangled in gossip. When women wanted to read their fortunes in coffee grounds, I left the room. My friends knew that for me that was not being faithful to God, and they respected me for it. It was frustrating that they had very little interest in talking about faith issues or matters of the heart, and I struggled, wondering whether I should be doing something more productive.

Sometimes they would ask me about our child-rearing, for we were seeking to have godly standards for our children. From their point of view, this was quite different from their general lack of discipline for their children. After years of togetherness and wondering whether our lives had had any impact, I was shocked when our neighbors' now-grown daughter told me that when she had children, she wanted to raise them like we did. She also gave me a special honor according to a local custom. When a couple is about to be married, they ask the happiest person they know to make their wedding bed in their new home. I was so touched that she asked me to do it! Still, my heart longed for them to understand the reason for my joy.

Growing in Jesus

Looking back now, I see more clearly how the Lord used those early years to deepen my faith, and I often remarked that the Lord did more *in* me than *through* me. How grateful I am that the Lord's love took me to a place where I could best grow in my own faith as I questioned, waited and found comfort in passages of Scripture that ministered hope to my heart. Our adopted country was the best place for me to grow in ways that I do not think I would have grown if we'd stayed in the States.

Over the course of time, I learned that finding my significance in Christ was not the same as how the world looks at significance. To live in His grace as His beloved child is hard at times with the constant supply of doubts and worldly viewpoints around us. I discovered my significance was not in a role or in how well I did. My significance was in being a child of God.

As I look back on my life, I am grateful for the rich truths of Scripture that have been my anchors in the midst of uncertainty. I love the picture of the canopy of His goodness and love over me when I read:

> Over everything the glory will be a canopy. It will be a shelter and shade from the heat of the day and a refuge and hiding place from the storm and rain. (Isa. 4:5-6)

I want to live in that place of refuge within His boundaries for me as a believer. Over time, I have come to see that the truths of Scripture that I memorize or know so well are the "tent pegs" holding me under the canopy:

> You will keep in perfect peace those whose minds are steadfast, because they trust in you. Trust in the LORD forever, for the LORD, the LORD himself, is the Rock eternal. (Isa. 26:3-4)

My part of that promise of peace is my choice to keep and seek a steadfast mind, one believing truth about the character of God.

People often ask whether we were afraid of living in in a Muslim country. Most of the time, I could truthfully say that apart from the horrific traffic, and from the potential for accidents from reckless drivers, I wasn't afraid. We kept a watchful eye in our circumstances, but we didn't live with life-and-death fear as there is in other fields. There were two times, though, that my courage and faith were tested. The first one was in December 1994 (I know the date because it is marked in my Bible), when Peter was asked to speak about Christianity on a radio station run by a Muslim minority group. The second time was when Peter was exposed on a national TV show that was advertised as a documentary but was actually a sensational exposé.

Over the years, people asked us about concerns for our children. Were they missing out on the opportunities they could have had in America? Did they like it in our adopted country? What about their schooling? On the whole, I think growing up overseas was a great time in their lives. They have a rich of appreciation for many cultures, foods, languages, travel, and friends that a life back home would never have given them. They have also seen the Great Commission (Matthew 28:16–20) lived out in our family and ministry.

A New Calling

After more than twenty-five years in our adopted country, Peter and I sensed that it was time to explore leaving there to broaden our ministry. We prayed and wrestled in our hearts to be open to God's leading. In the midst of our praying for direction, Peter and I had breakfast at a conference with a longtime colleague who was twenty years our senior. Peter, in a moment of inspiration, asked our friend what advice he had for us. He immediately said, "Every day I must consciously choose to make decisions that aren't based on comfort, convenience, or control. It is easy to let those factors lead my decision making, and they are self-serving." He didn't know we were in the throes of making this huge decision to uproot from our home of twenty-five years. Those were wise words to live by, and not just for this time in our lives. As Peter and I talked about this, we added another *c* word to that list — we didn't want to coast in life.

After a year of seeking wisdom and counsel, we moved to the UK to work with others who had a similar ministry training and overseeing field leaders. We were starting over as newbies again, but at least this time we knew the language! We enjoyed being with colleagues who were in the same season of life. Peter called these years of training, writing, and oversight his sweet spot. We were being used by the Lord in the very areas that all our years on the field had prepared us for. But we experienced challenges and frustrations unexpectedly, as we encountered problems with our visas. Eventually we had to leave. This was hard.

Nearly a year to the date of our departure from the UK, we moved to a country in continental Europe. We were rookies on the field once again and even needed to learn a new language. From our base in Europe, we are continuing with our training ministry, our oversight of teams, and especially our peacemaking ministry. God has placed us in a community of fellow caregivers with multiple agencies. We are waiting to see His glory as we are stretched to see the Lord use our peacemaking training in broader circles than what we had ever envisioned.

I have learned to live more at peace in my heart with the mystery of God. I am often reminded of Romans 11:33–36, which is Paul's doxology after he teaches doctrine that isn't always so easy to understand. There are some unknowns for our faith.

> Oh, the depths of the riches of the wisdom and knowledge of God! How unsearchable his judgments, and his paths beyond tracing out!
> "Who has known the mind of the Lord? Or who has been his counselor?"
> "Who has ever given to God, that God should repay him?"
> For from him and through him and for him are all things. To him be the glory forever! Amen.

Paul announces that God's judgments are unsearchable and His ways are inscrutable. Asking why just isn't the right course for my soul. I am choosing to land on the firm foundation that my God is sovereign and good, and His will may not always make sense this side of eternity.

So, until we know otherwise, we will dwell in this new land with our eyes on our King. He has led us so faithfully, and we are watching all the way until the day we will behold Him face to face and fully see His glory. When I ponder our more than thirty years overseas, I sometimes wonder whether my life has made a difference or impact for the gospel that makes it all seem worth it. We saw some fruit, but not nearly what we longed for. I have learned not to ask the world's usual question of "Were you successful?" for that is not the question that Jesus would want me to ask. We all long to hear "Well done, good and faithful servant" when we meet Him. My heart is most encouraged by Revelation 17:14:

> They will wage war against the Lamb, but the Lamb will triumph over them because he is Lord of lords and King of kings—and with him will be his called, chosen, and faithful followers.

May I be found worthy of being a follower like this.

10

Serving in Quiet Humility

Lorraine Loomans

Lorraine Loomans and her husband, Maurie,
*have been friends ever since my wife, Sharon, and I joined Col-
lege Hill Presbyterian Church in 1969. It has been one of the
greatest privileges of my life to watch these two servants of Jesus
follow their Lord with passion, wisdom, joy, energy and humility. They have always been so warm and kind to me as a younger, growing member of Jesus' family.*

*Lorraine serves behind the scenes in her work and ministry.
She is not an up-front person. She served families and children
in the College Hill community for many years and thus she has
fulfilled the calling of Jesus to serve those in need. Just observing
her in this role has been a challenge to my life. Lorraine has
served with gentleness and kindness for all and she is always
ready with a word of encouragement and support. Although
quiet in demeanor, she embodies such great and godly wisdom in
her thinking and behavior.*

*Even through the recent passing of her beloved husband,
Lorraine has been a tower of strength. She has lived out the ab-
solute hope that followers of Christ have as we are called home to
heaven. Through tremendous loss and certainly lots of tears,*

Lorraine has kept serving, praying, and encouraging. She is a dear saint, and it has been a privilege to call her a friend and fellow servant of our great King.

Lorraine's Story

Life began for me on a four-hundred-acre farm in Wisconsin. It was about five miles from the edge of town. My parents were "proper" Christians. The Bible was read at lunch and dinner. Pop was an elder, and for most of my young years we attended a small Reformed church with about one hundred members. Our minister, or dominie, as we called him, was the only college-educated person in our church. We had limited friends at church and some friends scattered throughout the city. Racine, Wisconsin, is an industrial city, so most of the men were factory workers. The moms stayed home with the children.

The farm my father managed was directly across from the county home for the aged, chronically ill, and anyone who needed care. Our yard was large, with beautiful oak trees and a lot of places to play! Our house was set back about a quarter of a mile from Green Bay Road, with the mailbox at the roadside.

Our name is a good Dutch name, Tunistra. When the people from the county home went for a walk, if they were Dutch, they would see the name on the mailbox and come into the house for a visit. They wanted to find out just what part of Holland we were from! Mom, an extrovert, loved the interaction and invited them in for coffee on Thursdays. As time went by, being a good baker, she served goodies with the coffee! The group was mostly men, and they would listen to a few verses from the Bible, and Mom prayed, if there was any need. This happened for many years. Early in my life, I learned to love and serve those who struggled in life.

I was the third child of eight. Besides the farm work, we learned to trust God. I loved athletics and with my oldest brother, Floyd, played baseball. It was great! My mom became ill, and I stayed home during what would have been my high school years. Because of the lack of money, at age sixteen, I started working at the Teleoplic Company as a time-bomb maker. This was toward the end of World War II. Later, I went to work for Johnson's Wax in the factory. I had good fun with great coworkers. Eventually, with encouragement from the management at Johnson's, I went to Central College in Iowa to pursue a degree in education.

Marriage, Graduate School, Children, and Procter & Gamble

Shortly after my graduation, I met Maurie at my church. He was from Wisconsin Rapids and was attending the University of Wisconsin, pursuing a degree in biology. During that summer, he worked at Johnson's Wax too. Like me, Maurie was raised in the Reformed church, and he sought out my church while he was in town. We fell in love and were married the next year.

My dad had a younger sister named Sue. She was just eight years older than my brother Floyd and lived with my family from time to time. She felt very close to our family and so did the man she married, George. Upon completion of Maurie's degree at the University of Wisconsin, Uncle George and Aunt Sue took Maurie and me on a trip to California. While in California, George wanted to stop to visit with his Aunt Nelly, who was a great Christian lady. During our initial conversation, she looked at Maurie and asked him, "As a young man, what do you plan to do for God?" This really made quite an impression on both of us, as you will come to see.

After five years of Maurie's graduate school, we wanted a good-paying job, to buy a house, to have children and to enjoy life! Even though we were both Christians, we had not thought of full-time Christian work. Maurie was hired at Procter & Gamble in Cincinnati. I think his parents were disappointed, as their dream was for Maurie to become a pastor. Maurie's uncle had drowned in Lake Michigan when he was a freshman at Hope College in preparation for the ministry. His parents really wanted Maurie to fill his uncle's place.

Maurie enjoyed his research at Procter & Gamble. We had our son Gary, bought a house and looked forward to another child. However, our second child died of complications at birth. The doctor recommended that we not have any more children and encouraged us to think about adoption.

In the midst of this time, we were looking for a church home and joined College Hill Presbyterian Church. Soon I joined to the Rebecca Circle and discovered several ladies who had adopted children. I made friends quickly, in particular with a wonderful woman named Anne. Anne had an adopted son and was about to adopt her second child, a daughter. She called to pick me up for the next circle meeting. Her adoptive children were beautiful. I was excited. So we pursued adoption and adopted a beautiful little girl who was eleven months old, named Julianne.

Two years later we adopted a wonderful six-week-old boy, Daniel.

The Call to Ministry and Service

Maurie and I were invited to join a committee searching for a youth pastor. After working on this committee, we began to feel like the church needed to develop better communication processes. In response to this need, the church hired Dr. Gary Sweeten. He had started a counseling program at a local university. He taught that a warm relationship with God was the answer to deep emotional problems and he started a number of ministries at College Hill. One that I became involved with was the Thursday 30 group.

What an awakening it was for me to find more of God's love and to learn that if I walked with Him, He could use me. God was really real! Dr. Sweeten, or Gary, as we called him, taught us many counseling skills. He changed my life. I had always loved people and loved helping people. Now I finally had a skill set to aid me in my heart's desire.

Martha was my first assignment. Pat, Gary's secretary, interviewed those seeking counseling and matched them with a compatible counselor. Martha was in her mid-fifties. She was full of vim and vigor, a real spitfire, and was born without a hand. Her husband passed away some months prior to her coming to us. Her doctor recommended that she call the Teleios Center since it was a free service and we could counsel her through depression. She was nervous at our first meeting, during which I discovered that Martha had several issues. She and her husband had owned and operated a TV repair shop, but her husband had been ill for some time and bedridden, so the business closed. Her home needed repair. Her cat was sick. She was feeling overwhelmed and depressed.

I asked Martha several questions. "Are you a Christian, Martha?" She replied, "Oh hell no! Do I have to be a Christian to be here?" I replied that she didn't have to be a Christian and explained to her how the center worked in connection with the church. I asked if she would like to come again after our session together and she replied that she would indeed like to come again. I inquired whether she owned a Bible. "No" was the answer. I gave her one to read and suggested that she read the Gospel of John.

To end our session, she agreed to let me pray for her. I specifically asked God that she be released from her depression, that her air conditioner would be repaired, and that somehow she would find the money for her cat to go to the veterinarian. Together we prayed for these things and she left feeling somewhat encouraged and excited about her return visit.

Well, Martha returned the following week and had several good reports. Upon returning home, Martha turned on the air conditioner, and lo and behold, it was working again! Not only that, but her cat was better. She was very happy that God answered our prayers but had one very funny question for me: "Lorraine, why would a great God make all those pigs run into the sea?" She was referring to the New Testament story of the demons leaving a man and going into the herd of swine and running directly down the hill into the sea.

Martha needed help long after this encounter and had many questions. We became good friends. I helped her with doctor visits and drugstore trips, and we often had lunch together. She had a wonderful sense of humor. She joined our church but she was worried that people would wonder why she didn't put money in the collection plate each week.

As time went on, Martha's health declined, and eventually she needed a powered wheelchair to remain mobile. College Hill Presbyterian Church was a fun and wonderful church to work with! Our business manager said we could collect the money, but we had to find someone to put down the first $500. I thought, *No problem!* One Sunday, I told a friend of Martha's what she needed and to please drop the money into the collection plate earmarked for Martha. Well wouldn't you know it! We received the exact amount needed for the purchase of that powered wheelchair. Within months, Martha saw God's love at work and above all felt it in her heart. She called me and said, "God showered me with love today. I gave my heart to Him!" With that she confirmed that she had committed her life to Christ!

During Martha's working years, she was a crossing guard. She needed to retire. Martha's wish was that she had worked for a big company so she could have a retirement party. This was a little bit of a challenge, but we reserved the recreation room in the home where she lived. The ladies at College Hill Presbyterian Church did the rest and gave her a retirement party to remember!

We had to say a final goodbye at Christmastime as she stepped into eternity. I am never sure who was more blessed, Martha or me. Her life was filled with joy, as is mine for having known her.

Her legacy and God's blessings continued to shower down on people all around. She never had children, so her brother, as her heir, gave her car to the Evangelical Presbyterian Church. The trustees then sold it and gave the money to the Missions Committee. The committee intern donated it to the Indian Gospel Mission. Shortly thereafter Maurie and another good friend visited the mission in India. Maurie was introduced to the woman who received the funds from the sale of the car, which enabled her to become part of the staff for this mission agency. When Maurie reached out to shake her hand, he discovered that she too was born without a hand! The ironies and grace of the loving mystery of God.

11

Equipping God's People

Gary Sweeten

My relationship with Gary started in 1973 *when he joined the staff of College Hill Presbyterian Church as the director of Christian education. Over the next few years we worked together on what became known as the Christian Lay Academy. This was the ministry of discipling adults for their calling. The church developed courses on the Bible, theology, and Christian living. At its peak of ministry, the Christian Lay Academy was teaching ten courses each quarter on different days and nights of the week. Thousands of adults went through these classes and were equipped to serve more effectively for the glory of Jesus. Gary was the staff leader for the ministry, and I was the dean. Gary's contribution in this was to give overall direction and then release others to use their gifts. It was a great privilege to work with him.*

During this time, he mentored me and encouraged me to serve and teach. Even after he left College Hill in 1989, I continued to follow Gary's ministry. He started Equipping Ministries International, Lifeway Counseling Center and Sweeten Life Systems. We spent time together primarily when I sent people to him for counseling. He was always willing to help and gave me advice that I needed to be able to help others. His counsel was always biblical and Christ centered. Gary has an insight into the lives of people and how they can change that is very rare and certainly God given.

More recently my time with him has significantly increased. Gary, along with Gary Sallquist, also included in this book, and I have been meeting for lunch every four to six weeks for the past five years or so. We share prayer requests, celebrate God's goodness to each of us and our families and give our insights to help each of us serve more effectively in our ministries. These are incredibly rich times together, and I cherish them with all my heart. I am blessed and enriched by each meeting. Gary is a great gift from God in my life.

So Gary had to be part of this book. He is a man of God who has come through tough times in his family life, has been called by God to a lifetime of service and continues to grow and serve as a disciple of his Lord and Savior Jesus Christ.

Gary's Story

I was born in 1938 into a family with multiple troubles in Ina, Illinois, a town of about three hundred people. In 1933, my older brother, Donald Thomas, died after living for just three days. His death had a lifelong impact of grief and unsettling for my mother and father. In 1935, Maurice was born, and he became the center to my family—the hero who replaced a child who died. In contrast, I was a financial and emotional burden because of my father's illness and our poverty.

The Sweeten family dynamics were filled with contrast and conflict. My father was an angry man, and I never remember hearing an affirming word about me. This was the fruit of his family history. His father passed away when he was a baby. His stepfather rejected him and treated him as an intruder. Thus, my dad was a prime example of what a destructive childhood can produce. Because of his anger and significant health issues, he had little success in his working career, and the family lived in poverty. After Dad became a Christian and attended church he began to mellow and lose his angry edge.

From the age of seven until fourteen, the role I played in the family was caring for my maternal grandfather, whose health problems demanded constant attention. This brought meaning and fulfillment to my life. My grandmother, "Mom" Taylor, was the daughter of a pastor and deeply committed to Christ. She knew the Word and lived it out daily. Mom Taylor was gentle and caring especially for those who did not know her Lord and helped the poor in many ways.

Grandad Taylor became sick in 1945 and died in 1952, when I was a freshman in high school. My response to the death was to lose the role I had as a good Christian boy. That led to resentment, anger, and rebellion and brought me many troubles with school authorities. I graduated from high school in 1956 still carrying a lot of emotional baggage, which came out in drinking, smoking, and belligerence. The first two years after high school I worked in a factory because I was emotionally unprepared for college. The struggles continued through 1957, until God showed up in June 1958.

From Rebellion to Calling

Despite experiencing spiritual rebirth as a child of ten in 1948, I was not living like a Christian. Thankfully, God confronted me and called me back to Him. While I was driving to a saloon one night, God put the question before me just as Joshua put the question to Israel. He said, "Gary, choose this day whom will you serve!" In Joshua's day, the people responded: "We will serve the LORD." That was my response to Joshua 24:19–24 as well. I said, "Where else can I go, Lord. Only you have the words of life." Shortly after that, I heard the Lord say, "Quit your job and go to college!" In obedience I enrolled in the local community college. I also started to serve our church and get involved in Bible studies as a dedicated follower of Christ. It was then I saw how important it was to do what Romans 12:2 says: "Do not conform to the world, but be transformed by the renewing of your mind." Because of my former dependence on the approval of others, I had to learn how to depend on what God said not what people did or said.

I taught in a small county school after college and learned a lot about equipping students to help each other, and I saw that was the way to do discipleship. In 1961, Karen Mayer and I married. Karen was the key to my returning to graduate school at Southern Illinois University. I was miserable working for a racist principal, and she said, "Why not quit teaching and return to SIU?" I did and studied higher education and counseling, graduating in 1967 from a two-year master's program. I then accepted a position at the University of Cincinnati as Assistant Dean of Men and resident hall counselor at Sawyer Hall, with twelve resident advisers under my supervision. I later became associate dean and assistant vice provost, a role in which I oversaw various student groups. I began attending Bible and Life seminars with InterVarsity Christian Fellowship. The focus on inductive applications of the Scripture opened my eyes to a new way to learn what the Bible was teaching.

At first Karen and I attended a Baptist church, but they were not open to my style of inductive Bible teaching. The leaders asked me to stop teaching and resign from my position in the church. We decided to leave the church in order not to cause more misunderstanding and conflict. As a result, we met Bob Loreaux, who discipled Karen and me in a small group setting. The group modeled a rich spiritual life of study and application. Bob went further and took me to visit the sick. He showed me how to pray for people, which helped me apply the Bible to practical needs in life and to care for and counsel them.

I enjoyed studying in small groups and saw the impact that face-to-face gatherings had on people. I wanted to use my counseling skills and biblical knowledge to help young people grow emotionally and spiritually. Since most churches were not open to inductive Bible studies or the application of the Bible in small groups, we looked for other ways of "being the church." The Jesus Movement on campus was brining many students to Christ who desperately needed the love and truth of Jesus. In response we established a house church across from the campus for the students. Many of the young people were deeply broken and in bondage to drugs, sex, and emotional distress. Our little church fellowship became a center for those hungry for salvation and healing. Karen and I were overwhelmed with the depth of need we saw every day on campus and in our home. As a result, I started a doctoral program in counseling to learn more about growth and healing.

During this time Francis Schaeffer had an enormous impact on my theological ideas. He taught me about how the power of God could bring real change to individuals, churches, and an entire culture. Schaeffer integrated the presence of God into his worldview and encouraged Christians to face and engage the culture without fear or hesitation. His book, *How Should We Then Live?*, contrasts the culture and the church. He unapologetically believed God is sovereign over and the author of all truth. He saw humans as fallen and living in bondage, rebellion and guilt. He articulated a Reformed view of humanity in desperate need of the redemption of God. He understood that God must do it all. God's work brings healing, holiness and freedom from shame. I was eager to hear Dr. Schaeffer's point of view, since many conservative Christians railed against people like me who were in the field of psychology.

Calling to College Hill Presbyterian Church

God brought a wonderful surprise to me when my University of Cincinnati colleague Dick Towner brought Dr. R. C. Sproul and Pastor Jerry Kirk from College Hill Presbyterian Church to campus to share with students. I was impressed with these terrific leaders and later joined Dr. Kirk on the Billy Graham Committee. In 1973, he asked me to prayerfully consider joining the College Hill Presbyterian Church staff as Christian education director. Karen and I spent a weekend in prayer about the opportunity. I would have to leave my position at the university, with a planned sabbatical to finish my doctorate. It was a difficult decision, but we clearly heard God was calling us to leave my career in higher education to become part of the adventure of a full-time ministry in a large church.

The minister of Christian education was responsible for Sunday school, youth groups, and adult Bible studies from the cradle to the grave. I quickly saw that equipping adults to be better parents and Christian leaders was the key to lasting change. My team of volunteers and I started the Christian Lay Academy to carry out the new vision. Eventually the academy offered about forty courses each year on the Bible and theology, parenting, small group dynamics, and renewing the mind. Hundreds of College Hill Presbyterian Church members and members from other churches attended.

Not everyone supported the inclusion of practical courses such as parenting and active listening in the curriculum. Some wanted to restrict the teaching to the Bible and creeds. Since that was not my interest or conviction, I considered leaving the position and the people I loved. The church was marked by a rare joy and freedom in Jesus that we craved. I felt affirmed and was glad to become part of the staff. It was wonderful to see people grow in Jesus and have Christians ministering to each other. However, if I could not do what I believed God had called me to do, I would leave. I was offered the position of dean of students at Gordon-Conwell Theological Seminary. It was exactly what my training had prepared me for—but thankfully God intervened again. Pastor Jerry Kirk and a key elder, Bob Rumford, came up with a different plan. As a result, I remained at

College Hill to undertake a new position of Christian discipleship that focused on enhancing family life, developing small groups and promoting and expanding the current healing ministry.

The new call grew into what we called the Teleios Ministry (*teleios* means to be whole in Christ). We offered additional care and counsel to individuals and families. We offered care for people suffering from mental, emotional, and relational problems. I received a Doctorate in Counselor Education from the University of Cincinnati in 1975 and began to implement my insights at church. My dissertation focused on the psychological research on how empathy, warmth, and caring can be integrated with the fruit of the Holy Spirit. The title was "Development of a Systematic Human Relations Model for Evangelical Churches." This work was the product of my belief that all of God's people, who are saved by the work of Jesus, need to grow into wholeness and that church members can be trained as helpers, lay pastors, and mentors.

Equipping the Saints

Paul's message to the Ephesians is the key to my life purpose and ministry:

> So Christ himself gave the apostles, the prophets, the evangelists, the pastors and teachers, to equip his people for works of service, so that the body of Christ may be built up until we all reach unity in the faith and in the knowledge of the Son of God and become mature, attaining to the whole measure of the fullness of Christ.

Then we will no longer be infants, tossed back and forth by the waves, and blown here and there by every wind of teaching and by the cunning and craftiness of people in their deceitful scheming. Instead, speaking the truth in love, we will grow to become in every respect the mature body of him who is the head, that is, Christ. From him the whole body, joined and held together by every supporting ligament, grows and builds itself up in love, as each part does its work. (Eph. 4:11-16)

As a teacher within the body of Christ, my calling is to equip others for service. Every believer has spiritual gifts, so I aimed to call forth those gifts, releasing church members to do the work of ministry. Believing that trained church helpers can usually be as effective as professionals, I collaborated with others in producing training resources such as Listening for Heaven's Sake and Apples of Gold 1 and 2. Over the years, we had over fifty lay counselors, who saw people who struggled with anxiety, depression, eating disorders, pornography, same-sex attraction, and marriage and family conflicts. Our church mission was to be an equipping center, so Rev. Ron Rand and I started having seminars and workshops on implementing Ephesians 4 for local ministers. The seminars grew in reputation and size, with attendees coming from all over America and some foreign nations. We printed our materials, and they became the cornerstone of Equipping Ministries International, the organization we founded in 1978 at the urging of our church trustees. Over four thousand people went through our courses such as Listening for

Heaven's Sake, Rational Christian Thinking and Breaking Free.

Ministry Around the World

I am honored and humbled that God allowed me to train so many members of the church around the world through Equipping Ministries International. One notable experience occurred at a 1987 retreat to equip leaders in Norway. Together with a small team of Teleios workers, we taught them about caring, empathy, listening, and healing prayer. Kjell Aanensen, the chief evangelist of the YMCA for Norway, came deeply depressed and seeking a touch from Jesus. Our message of healing in Christ sounded great and he was the first to volunteer for prayer in the small group led by Elder Larry Chrouch. God miraculously lifted his depression and his life completely changed. Kjell went on to serve as the head of Teleios Norway. He also travels internationally with the message of hope. Amazingly, his ministry has included training over six thousand evangelists and lay counselors in Mongolia!

A key passage for us was Philippians 3:12–14:

> Not that I have already obtained all this, or have already arrived at my goal, but I press on to take hold of that for which Christ Jesus took hold of me. Brothers and sisters, I do not consider myself yet to have taken hold of it. But one thing I do: Forgetting what is behind and straining toward what is ahead, I press on toward the goal to win the prize for which God has called me heavenward in Christ Jesus.

This passage describes the reality of all Christians, certainly including myself. We have not yet attained what we are to be in Jesus, but we press on to make it our own. This is the process of sanctification. It is a lifelong process of growing in righteousness. My role is to help those who are pressing on, to train and equip them for the glory of Christ. An important part of this process is to understand the wounds of the past and to grow beyond them in health and wholeness. The process enables people to be freed from the bondage, rebellion, guilt, and shame of their past and to move in health, joy, peace, and love into their God-given lives of service. Jesus' death on the cross paid for our sins and freed us from the brokenness of our lives, including our past.

I am grateful for the church. What I emphasize is that the church is not the place for the righteous but for sinners who have been saved by grace. It is open to all who are committed to the Lordship of Jesus. The church is the place for all to grow in being more Christ-like with godly caring, sharing, and prayer. The Word of God is the basis for all we do, think, and say. The church is the most powerful therapeutic healing community ever established in history. It is a place for every member to use their gifts to serve others.

Another amazing story comes from a scholar who headed the New Testament Department of Norway's largest evangelical seminary. This man was a brilliant teacher of the Word of God, but his life was filled with anger and bitterness. His inner state had impacted his health and caused his body to be covered with eczema for years. His students and family cowered before him because of his anger. His initial response to our teaching was negative.

After dinner, he angrily confronted me with the charge that it was not biblical, Norwegian, or Lutheran!

I said, "Let's go to your small group so I can listen to your concerns." I attended his group, and we all listened to the story of his rejection and betrayal for over two hours. It had happened twenty-four years before, but the memories were still vivid and fresh in his heart. We asked him to confess his bitterness and ask God for healing, and he did. Then we all prayed for him. Through the power and presence of the Holy Spirit and listening in love with God's grace, radical changes were produced in his life. The next day his wife asked what I had done because her husband was so radically changed. I simply said that it was not what I had done but what God had done. His eczema was almost totally healed as well!

> When I kept silent, my bones wasted away.
> (Ps. 32:3)

IMI Church in Stavanger is the largest church in Norway. Pastor Martin Cave built the church to be a Teleios equipping center. It has grown in numbers, impact, and encouragement in a culture of spiritual death. It has over 150 churches in a network in Norway. Its school trains one hundred youth each year from all over the world. In the last ten years, it has led about ten thousand people to Christ and planted two hundred churches in Cambodia.

Continuing Ministry Expansion

I left College Hill in 1989 to start Lifeway Counseling Center. Our goal was to bring together the best of Christian ministry and Christian worldview, with excellent professional psychiatric and psychological expertise. These professions are not enemies of the Christian faith. Their skills, research, and training can be used within the context of biblical teaching to bring healing to those who are hurting and in need of professional help. The counselors at Lifeway have been used mightily by God to help thousands of individuals, families, and marriages. To God be the glory!

I also wanted to expand Equipping Ministries International. This gave me the privilege of expanding our national and international equipping to other nations. Our teams served in South Africa, Scandinavia, Russia, Singapore, and Africa. God brought a wonderful team of gifted leaders to Equipping Ministries International who have continued the work with ever-increasing impact long after I left in 1994. The ministry has produced outstanding training resources that have been used around the world. These resources have been translated into many languages and have been used to train thousands of church and ministry leaders. Equipping Ministries International's goal is to bring the wholeness, peace, and joy that Jesus promises to God's people by overcoming past hurts, shame, guilt, and brokenness. God's instruments to wholeness work! Listening, caring, sharing, and the renewing of the mind bring great blessing. The foundation for much of the work was the teaching on active listening, caring, and sharing that was started at College Hill.

I have had the privilege of working with church and ministry teams with the goal of increasing their effectiveness and unity. I have found that many pastors and leaders are desperate for the kind of training that my experiences with Equipping Ministries International,

College Hill and Lifeway Counseling can bring. Many are also struggling personally with fulfilling their calling to ministry. It is heartbreaking to hear the stories of pastors and leaders who are struggling with depression and disappointment. What a blessing to see them grow into greater wholeness and service to King Jesus!

Since leaving Equipping Ministries International, I founded Sweeten Life Systems to focus on training, counseling, and discipleship of pastors and Christian leaders. We do not provide a system of care and counsel ourselves but train churches and community organizations to use tools to do their ministry more effectively. For example, we are training mentors for children in the public schools in Cincinnati. The need for mentors for thousands of schoolchildren in Cincinnati is desperate. So many come from broken homes where they get little or no support. They often struggle with behavioral issues, are not motivated to study and learn and too often are considering self-harm, including suicide. Mentors offer a listening and caring heart and ear. They have a lifelong impact on the lives of their students. We are training more and more mentors each year and it is wonderful to see how they are used for God's blessing of young people who have little support at home.

We continue to support the work we began in Russia in 1990. My sister in Christ, Dr. Galina Chentsova, MD, came to Cincinnati to be trained with the Equipping Ministries International materials. She integrates them with her professional training as a psychiatrist. She has been used powerfully by God in helping many come to wholeness in Jesus and leave addiction behind. The work in Russia took our team there many times to establish the model. Decades of communist atheism produced millions of depressed people with little hope or joy. Many suffer from post-traumatic stress disorder, with high rates of alcoholism and drug abuse.

Our latest outreach ministry focuses on equipping caregivers with the biblical wisdom, skills, and understanding we practiced at College Hill Presbyterian Church and Equipping Ministries International. There are over forty million adults with a loved one who suffers from a disability or chronic illness. Sweeten Life Systems has developed a separate ministry called Family EQ. It is an online equipping system available to overworked caregivers twenty-four hours a day to reduce their stress and empower them to provide better care.

I still am amazed that God has taken a rebel from a very small town in Illinois and has been able to use him around the world, through many ministries, to touch the lives of His people. I am clearly an example of what our extraordinary God does with ordinary people. To Him be all the glory!

12

Transforming Lives and the Culture

Ford Taylor

I was first introduced to Ford Taylor more
*than twenty years ago. He and Jerry Kirk were members of a
small group of Christian leaders from Cincinnati called City
Servants. Jerry shared with me how anointed Ford was in training others so that they could be more effective in serving God's
Kingdom. Soon after Jerry shared this with me, I had the privilege of meeting personally with Ford. I found him to be a dear
brother in Christ, with great humility, and incredible gifts and
skills.*

*Since I first met Ford, my wife, Sharon, and I have had the
blessing of going through all three days of Transformational
Leadership training twice. We have been blessed each time and
have learned so much about personal, organizational, and ministry change. God has given Ford real insight into these issues. He
starts with three biblical principles—unconditional love, unconditional forgiveness, and dangerous transparency. The training
is straight from God's Word. It is practical, clear, and easy to
apply in everyday life. Maybe we are just slow learners, but both*

Sharon and I look forward to going through the training again. It is that good!

Over the past four or five years, my relationship with Ford has deepened in two important ways. First, we have begun to pray for each other on a daily basis. In addition, when our schedules permit, Sharon and I have begun to meet for dinner every three or four months with Ford and his wife, Sandra, and Jerry and Patty Kirk. These are times of deep sharing, caring and, fellowship.

My hope is that you will be encouraged by Ford's journey through depression and insecurity, sin, and brokenness, to being used by our extraordinary God in amazing ways. What a blessing it has been for me to see how Transformational Leadership has been used around the world for the glory of Christ.

Ford's Story

I was born in 1957 in Paris, Texas, and came from a great family. I was called to live up to high expectations. This created a sense of needing to work and find my value in what I did in school, sports, or whatever else, and never really feeling like I was good enough, even though my parents loved me and told me that I was. They were strong believers and had us in church every week, and I have the pins to show I didn't miss church for thirteen years in a row!

The practice of the Christian faith was essentially a list of do's and don'ts, primarily the don'ts. My parents had good business sense and were committed to quality and service. They always worked hard to do better to provide for our family and were generous to those around us.

I came to Christ as a five-year-old. My pastor was convinced it was a real conversion, not just something to please my parents or to measure up to social expectations. When I was ten years old, I made a commitment to never smoke cigarettes, do drugs, or drink alcohol as my list of don'ts. In high school, I was president of the junior class and also president of the student body. Discipleship was a strong theme in my life, and I was co-leader for the junior high and high school youth group in our church, with an emphasis on personal change and evangelism. This was part of my desire to please others through performance.

Through my success in school and church youth group, I had a fairly good Christian walk and maintained my commitments to the don'ts. At the same time, I had a lot of insecurities and unresolved issues, one of them being caused by my being sexually abused by a female schoolteacher in grade school. I was filled with anger and depression. At the age of seventeen, I had a significant and real encounter with God. I had a sense of a calling to the unity of the church, which is something that is unusual for a Baptist. I shared this sense of calling with my pastor, and he said that he didn't believe that God wanted me to do that.

There was an annual mission trip for the youth group that I had participated in a number of times. During my junior year, as I was praying about the trip, I had a sense that I was not supposed to go. My pastor said that God would not tell me that.

But God was very clear: "Don't go."

Based on that clarity, I decided to stay back and not go early with the setup team, and to go later with the larger group, and seek clarity on why He would say not to go.

As it turned out, I was in the hospital having an emergency appendectomy at the same time the original crew was on the plane. When I got out of the hospital, I grabbed many of the students who could not afford to go on the trip, and we had a weeklong mission trip right there in our city. I heard for years from so many people how their children were affected that summer and how the students who did not get to go away didn't feel left out when the ones who did go returned. They had their own stories to tell of what happened.

There was now more pain because the pastor still did not recognize that God was speaking to me. Many years later, I was at my nephew's wedding. When I walked in, I was told that my pastor from back then was there and that he wanted to see me. It had been over thirty years since I had seen him. He looked at me with tears in his eyes and said, "I am so sorry. I just didn't know back then what I know now." That was a very healing moment. I was very surprised that he even remembered all of those conversations about how I felt God visited and spoke to me.

The College Years

I attended Texas A&M, and as a freshman I again had a strong sense of God directing me. Again, I resisted. There was a slow fade away from God during my sophomore year. I did not have a nurturing mentor during what had happened to me from the ages of five to nineteen. Looking back, I would have pursued a mentor to disciple me.

I met Sandra, my future wife, during my senior year, when she was a freshman. I graduated in 1979 and stayed in College Station, where I managed some local sporting goods stores, waiting for her to graduate. This was natural for me because I had worked in a sporting goods store in high school, and I also was the assistant manager of that store during college. In both cases, I had great mentors. Sandra and I got married in 1981, when she was a junior.

We did not to have children for many years because we were busy working to build our business. We had differences in theology, as I had been raised Baptist and Sandra had been raised Catholic. We could have made a movie or sitcom over our differences! When our oldest daughter was born, we compromised and started attending an independent, Bible-based church. I would now call it an evangelical church.

Amazing Business Success but Personal Trouble

In 1982, I started a career in business. I bought C.C. Creations, a company that was near bankruptcy. Its bank asked me if I would take on the debt and try to fix it. It was a very small company that screen-printed T-shirts, number stickers, and hand-painted signs. Even though the company had a very bad reputation, I was only twenty-five and thought I could do anything. I discovered that it was not going to be easy. I became discouraged and didn't believe the company was going to be able to overcome their bad reputation. I called my parents and told them that I thought that we would have to close the company. They told me to sleep on it, pray about it, and see what happened.

The next day, I developed a sales pitch that convinced customers to give us another try. "I will sit right here until you give us an order to give us another chance. If we mess up, you will never hear from me again." Along the way, the company became successful. Because of this success, I had the opportunity to meet and work with a venture capital group headquartered in Houston.

As the company grew, we became Brazos Sportswear and moved the corporate headquarters of the company to Cincinnati. We continued to acquire other companies and became one of the largest screen-printing and embroidering companies in the United States, with two thousand employees and $300 million in annual sales.

During a twenty-three-month period in 1995–1997, I commuted between Texas and Cincinnati. The business was growing, but I wasn't doing well. For one thing, I was prideful and arrogant, believing that I was God's gift to business. An even greater problem was that the travel created opportunities for unfaithfulness to Sandra, and I engaged in an extramarital affair. The bottom line is that running the business and the affair filled me with anger and depression.

We decided to move to Cincinnati in 1997 and began helping with a church plant. A semi-retired pastor, Dale Thorne, and his wife, Anita, took me under their wing. I started seeing a natural homeopathic chiropractor, Dr. Greg Pitman. It is not an overstatement to say that with their help and Sandra's unconditional forgiveness, they saved my life. Through their love, grace, and mercy I was able to overcome depression and suicidal thoughts.

Another Calling from God

I began to hear a call to the ministry. Sandra, too, heard God's new calling on my life. In light of my sin, how was this possible? God is amazing, patient, and good. The calling I felt was to the discipleship of God's people. The missing element that I perceived was the failure of God's people and the institutional church to fully grasp Romans 12:1–2:

> Therefore, I urge you, brothers and sisters, in view of God's mercy, to offer your bodies as a living sacrifice, holy and pleasing to God—this is your true and proper worship. Do not conform to the pattern of this world, but be transformed by the renewing of your mind. Then you will be able to test and approve what God's will is—his good, pleasing and perfect will.

Now there was a calling on my life and the vision that God had given me. In the midst of this I had a Damascus Road experience and heard the call again. I had said no to God's calling at ages seventeen and thirty-three. God made it clear that this was the last time He was going to ask. This time, the calling took.

In response to God's call I started a ministry called Transformation Cincinnati Northern Kentucky. Our mission statement is "God's people, business, churches, government, and schools be united through prayer, plans, and actions to spread the gospel of Jesus Christ throughout the city, region, country, and the world." While I was launching Transformation Cincinnati Northern Kentucky, I was also doing business consulting. One of my clients called me into his office and closed the door. He asked me,

"When you buy a company or consult with a company, how often do you get these results?"

I reluctantly said, "Every time."

He then asked me another question: "If that is the case, then why are you not using the training to change the city?"

I responded, "If those leaders really knew who I am, they would not follow me." He convinced me to bring a group of people together to do a leadership brain dump one day each month for six months. At the end of that training they told me it was the best thing they had ever been through, so we did it for another six months.

Eventually this training was put into a manual, which became the core of Transformational Leadership Training. Now, by God's grace, we have a team of people who do this training in different cities, countries, and organizations around the world. God is really good!

Key Characteristics of Training

Transformation Leadership Training provides cultural and classic consulting, executive coaching, conflict resolution, how to provide discipline, how to remove personal and organizational constraints, and team building. The training is offered to businesses and all types of organizations. The training is provided through classes as well as an online virtual interactive platform called TL on Demand.

Those who experience a Transformation Training Seminar tell me that the principles they especially appreciate are the dynamics of change and strategies to apply those dynamics: genuine affirmation of others, things to say and what not to say, learning how to apologize appropriately, background perspectives on the ways that people actually learn, and the best way to effectively approach others, which includes humility, caring, and kindness.

Almost all Transformational Leadership Training is two days long. However, when the participants are part of the Christian community, a vitally important third day is added. I call this the missing link. The first two days of training are based on this missing link, but day three makes the biblical foundation of the training explicit.

The problem, or what I call the missing link, is the reality that we don't love our neighbors as we love ourselves and we don't love ourselves as God does. We don't realize how much God loves us. We have spent hundreds of years making Christians and very little time making disciples. We are told to spread the gospel and make disciples among the nations. We are also told to preach the Kingdom and to expect signs and wonders to follow. But in reality, we have not preached the Kingdom, nor have we made disciple makers who are operating across all the spheres of the Kingdom.

It is hard to go out and make disciples if we have not been discipled ourselves. A true *transformational* disciple has the heart of a spiritual father or mother. That means they understand, teach, and live out unconditional love and unconditional forgiveness as Jesus taught them. When we have enough disciple makers like this, we will change the world because unconditional love and unconditional forgiveness do not walk in judgment or enablement but make more disciples.

The training works because God's principles of human interaction, which are unconditional love, unconditional forgiveness, and dangerous transparency are true! Christ taught and lived out these principles. Through them He shows us how to build and restore intimacy. These principles work in both secular and faith-based settings. They have been used in businesses, with government leaders, in the military, and in churches and ministries. God has opened the doors for the training to be used in many places in the United States and in India, the Philippines, Australia, the Netherlands, Germany, Brazil, and a number of African nations including Kenya, South Africa, Ethiopia, Rwanda, and Nigeria.

The impact of Transformational Leadership Training is often limited in Christian settings because too many Christians do not believe Romans 8:1:

> Therefore, there is now no condemnation for those who are in Christ Jesus.

They live in fear of men, fear of God as their judge, and believe that God is out to get them. Instead of believing these lies, we must learn to love ourselves the way God does. When we believe in God's freedom in Christ, He releases the power and presence of His Holy Spirit among us and amazing things happen to and through us as His people.

Transformation Leadership Impact

As the Transformation Leadership developed, God was busy shaping both me and the ministry. I recognized the leading of God for transformation in my marriage. Once I was leading a training on marriage, and just before I left the house to teach the event, I made a comment to Sandra. It was hurtful and wrong, and I saw Sandra's countenance change before my very eyes. After I arrived at the training, I turned around and headed home. I needed to apologize and ask for forgiveness. It was both humbling and humiliating, but it was what I needed to do. I am thankful that Sandra showed me grace, love, mercy, and forgiveness. I wish I would learn not to behave or speak in such a way that I need her to be Jesus with skin on for me so often!

In 2016, I was diagnosed with Lyme disease. I had little energy and almost no appetite, and I needed to rest almost all the time. Despite the physical struggle, I asked my doctor whether I could to fly to Ethiopia to do some training. He said, "Yes, I think it will be good for you to go based on what you are doing and your call to do it, if you will get lots of rest in between meetings."

So I went, and God showed up big time! There were fifty-three denominational leadership teams. We conducted the two days of training with materials in English and Amharic. At the end of the training one of the leaders stood up and looked at me and said: "I want to share something that I've never shared before. My story is the same as yours. I want my congregation to understand the grace of Jesus the same way people understand it when you share your story. I'm going to share that with my congregation this Sunday." Then three more leaders stood up and said the same thing. Then the leader who brought us to Ethiopia stood and said, "Men and women, if we would all share our stories in our churches this Sunday morning and beyond, we could start a revival that could not be stopped." All I can say is, Praise the Lord.

The training has been used powerfully in business settings many times. Britney Ruby Miller is the President of Jeff Ruby Culinary Entertainment. Here is what she has to say about the impact of Transformational Leadership training in the company she leads:

> Transformational Leadership has been absolutely pivotal for our entire company and my personal leadership growth as well. Looking back, the timing of when I first experienced Transformational Leadership was extremely fortuitous. Growing up and participating fully in a family business, I gained exceptional operations training, and truly had solid mentors along the way. However, in order to fully mature and really earn my position in the corporate office, I knew I was craving more business training.
>
> Ford Taylor and his training were both complete surprises that I can confidently say added more than I could have even dreamed. He became a role model, mentor, and supplemental father figure. He truly helped shape me into the President I am today. His tutelage was a *huge* factor that contributed to the following results (among others) since I took a leadership role in our company: we have doubled our number of restaurants, grown top line 22 percent, and also increased net income by 45 percent! Additionally, our employee retention rate is 25 percent better than the restaurant industry average—our people want to stay because of

the Transformational Leadership culture! I am thankful for Ford Taylor, Transformational Leadership, and all the permanent life benefits that both of them have made possible for me, my family, and my company.

We have been given the opportunity to do training within the United States Military Service. We have been blessed and thrilled to present Transformation Leadership Training to those who are protecting our country and are willing to give their lives for the freedom we enjoy. The response to the training has been stunning. Here is a selection of three statements of appreciation from those service people.

The skills taught can be applied to all aspects of life. This is by far the best training I have attended while working for the Department of Defense. Thank you for the opportunity to learn about myself and not be judged. (GS-13 Vectored)

None of the usual 'surface-level' training and discussion. Really open, honest environment that resonated deep inside, and offers real-world solutions/tools to enhance my work/home life. Among the very best training in my long career! (GS-14)

This course is a true reality check! Oftentimes, we think we're really doing quite well, but this course goes so much deeper to underpin the principles taught to make them enduring for true application. The openness of the instructor was amazing and greatly enhanced his and the course's credibility. (GS-13, Supervisor)

Beyond the military, Transformational Leadership Training has had a wonderful impact on marriage and families. One person who went through the training wrote me.

> If you knew us, you would have thought everything was great. Things looked wonderful from the outside, but we were slowly growing apart. I was the problem in my own marriage and I didn't even know it. I blamed my wife and work or anything other than myself. Transformational Leadership helped me find my blind spot and gave me the tools to change. I would not be the happily married and blessed man I am today without using these tools every single every day.

Ray and Linda Noah, lead pastors of Portland Christian Center, began boldly praying, "Lord, make us the greatest conduit for the Great Commission the world has ever seen." They say,

> It was soon after we began praying that prayer that we met Ford Taylor and were introduced to Transformational Leadership. Over the next several years we participated in forums and training sessions and began practicing Transformational Leadership principles. They gave

us a common language and created a pathway for us to be more usable and effective.

Today we use it to counsel married couples, lead our board, direct our ministry teams, and engage our congregation in difficult and challenging situations. We have witnessed the blessing of God as we lead according to His principles. God has helped us to lead our church to be 100 percent debt free, and missions giving has increased exponentially.

It has been amazing to me to see how God has used Transformational Leadership to bless so many lives around the world. He has done so despite all my sin and brokenness. Mine is the story of ordinary people being used by our extraordinary God. All praise and glory to Him.

13

Serving the Least of These

Beth Guckenberger

I have known members of the Guckenberger family and their work with Back2Back for more than ten years. My first introduction was to John and Corrie Guckenberger through Montgomery Community Church and their friendship with Brett, our second-oldest son, and his wife, Betsy. John was in the construction business, and it was very clear that he and Corrie had a heart for ministry and especially for third-world children. They shared with my wife, Sharon, and me their strong desire to leave the corporate world and enter into full-time vocational ministry. It was then that we learned of Back2Back and the incredible ways that God was using the ministry to serve the "least of these."

We were then introduced to John's identical twin brother, Todd, and his wife, Beth. How anyone tells the brothers apart is beyond me, but John says he is the good-looking one! Todd and Beth are the international founders, visionaries, and co-executive directors for Back2Back. They have huge hearts for God and love the children of the world.

Over the years I have seen the passion, commitment, and God-given gifts of all four Guckenbergers. The impact of

Back2Back in Mexico, Africa, the Dominican Republic, India, Haiti, and Cincinnati is simply "beyond what we could ask or imagine." They are serving children among the poorest of the poor. Most of these children are orphans. Their work is consistent with the heart of the Father and the ministry of Jesus.

More recently I have had the privilege of getting to know Beth much better. She has a huge heart, and her spiritual gifts are simply amazing. She is a marvelous speaker, a very strong leader, and a wonderful author. She has written nine books (and more on the way, I am sure). Sharon and a small group of her closest friends have been studying Beth's book Start with Amen. They have been blessed by it, and I know that you will be blessed by all her books.

Beth's story is not only a personal spiritual journey but is the story of Back2Back. I pray that you will be both challenged and blessed by it.

Beth's Story

I was born in 1972 in Indianapolis, have two brothers, and am the middle child. Dad worked for Dow Chemical, and he got transferred to Cincinnati in 1980. Church, faith, and ministry were at the center of our family life. Discipling others and neighborhood evangelism were not just talked about but were a daily practice. Mom and Dad were always close friends of our pastors, so I was regularly exposed to Christian leaders, ministers, and missionaries. They were part of a small group that planted Hope Church in 1990. My life was all about following and serving Jesus. How I was blessed!

My father was a godly follower of Jesus. However, at a relatively young age, he was diagnosed with cancer. I prayed for his complete healing, as did many others. I prayed, fasted, anointed with oil, and believed with all my might that God would heal him. However, God had other plans, and my father passed away at the age of fifty-one.

That God did not answer the prayers the way I wanted left a deep spiritual wound in my heart. I began to doubt that God was really good and that He heard and responded to the prayers of His people. The loss of my father created a crisis of faith for me.

Despite this heart wound toward God, I had a clear calling from Him to help "the least of these" from a very early age. Even as a teenager, God made it clear that this was going to be my ministry from and for Jesus. I met Todd, my husband, in high school through our participation in Young Life. It was thrilling to see that he had the same calling. So the ministry of Back2Back has been one of mutual love and service to children around the world ever since our high school days and even before.

Todd and I started dating when I was seventeen, and we both went to Indiana University. I majored in English and education, while Todd studied history and education. The truth be known, we both really majored in Campus Crusade! I graduated in 1994, one year ahead of Todd. We got married right after he graduated.

Todd and I started serving children with a mission trip to Monterey, Mexico, in 1995–1996. While in Monterey, we were introduced to children who were orphans living in poverty, without decent food, water, or medical care. Our sense of calling was to focus on meeting these physical needs. Jesus spoke clearly to us about serving others through Matthew 25.

After we returned home, we prayed about what more we could do. Again, the Lord spoke clearly to us. We decided to move to Monterey in the summer of 1997. We partnered with a children's home there and focused on service to children.

A dear friend of ours, Dain Jepson, had the same sense of calling. Even as he was an administrator at Cincinnati Hills Christian Academy, he had a heart for the children of Mexico. Our first year in Mexico was amazing, as over 350 people came on mission trips from various Cincinnati churches. The children were being cared for in wonderful ways, and there was a clear sense of the power of the Holy Spirit. In spite of this fruitful experience, we had no plans for what we might do after that first year.

It seemed wise to return to Cincinnati and get our act together. Todd joined the staff of Cincinnati Hills Christian Academy, while Dain left his job at the school and moved to Mexico with his family from 1998–2000. While in Cincinnati, Jeff Grear, a pastor at Hope Church, had an idea to start an organization where parachurch staff could come alongside church staff and together serve the local US church. He named his idea Back2Back.

When we saw the ministry grow in Mexico, we realized we were in need of an umbrella authority and structure, as well as a nonprofit status. We asked Jeff whether we could come under that name. He said yes, and Back2Back was born!

In 2000, we traded places with Dain. He moved back to Cincinnati to run the US office, while Todd and I settled into a long stint as missionaries in Monterey. We stayed in Mexico until 2014, when we felt called to return to Cincinnati and continue the development of the ministry into other countries. Since then we have seen God expand the work into Haiti, the Dominican Republic, Africa, India, and Mazatlan and Cancun in Mexico, and even here at home in Cincinnati. God is great, and He sure is good.

Openness to God's Way and Will

The adventure that we had prayed about took a dramatic turn in 1998. Our friends, the Jepson's, serving the children in Mexico, called to tell me about a four-year-old who had been hit by a car. They were at their wits' end and asked me to come and help. I immediately flew to Monterey. Over the next few weeks we worked through the challenges faced by the four-year-old and her family. Praise the Lord, the little girl was restored to complete health.

Not only did God want me in Mexico to help our dear friends, but He had an exciting surprise for me as well. I received a phone call from an adoption agency that told me about a seven-week-old boy whom we could adopt. While previously Todd and I had discussed the possibility, now the choice was right before us. Todd came down to Mexico the next day. We said yes and adopted Evan even though we already had Emma, our four-month-old daughter. After several weeks with Evan, we returned as a new family to Cincinnati.

Evan had significant health challenges, so we took him to Children's Hospital for an evaluation. The diagnosis was grim. Evan had a severe case of cerebral palsy with significant brain damage. We were told he would never walk or talk. The doctor asked whether we understood the challenges we were facing. I am sorry to say that I did not immediately organize a prayer team because of the death of my father and God's seeming unresponsiveness to those fervent prayers two years previous. I did know that others were praying, but I couldn't. I was still in deep spiritual pain about those who were closest to my heart.

In the months ahead, Evan received a lot of physical therapy, but he did not appear to be making much progress. He wasn't walking and had almost no ability to communicate with me. One day the physical therapist was at our home. She noticed that I picked Evan up whenever he began to cry or even struggle and told me that my behavior was not helpful. This really made me angry. However, I did choose to listen to her. And it made a difference! One day when he was struggling without my help, he pulled himself up on the couch and made his way over to his sister, Emma. This was delightfully shocking.

As I continued to restrain my instincts to rescue, he made great strides and started walking. One day he actually began to walk without holding on to anything. I was so excited to see this that I called Todd and then took both he and Emma to show him his amazing little boy. When we arrived and went into the school, I put Evan down on his feet, and he walked to his dad. The office staff, who had been so prayerfully encouraging and supportive, both cheered and cried!

God is really good!

By the time Evan was two years old, the doctors at Children's Hospital said that he was completely healed. In August 2000, we moved back to Mexico. At this point, there was no evidence that Evan had a problem. He started in public school and was playing soccer at the age of four. We stayed in Mexico for twelve years and began to feel like we could do the best job of developing the ministry of Back2Back from Cincinnati. Evan attended public school in a suburb of Cincinnati. In high school, he gave up soccer and began to play football, excelling as a wide receiver! After graduating from high school, he attended Taylor University and was a standout on the football team.

Seeing God's blessing and healing for Evan healed the spiritual wound in my heart from the death of my father. I learned and accepted that God is God and I am not. I began to believe and celebrate that God is sovereign, trustworthy, and good.

The ministry of Back2Back began to grow quickly. Every staff member was expected to raise their own support. The qualification for our staff was really simple: be a follower of Jesus, sold out to His Kingdom through serving orphans, leaders, and volunteers in helping the "least of these." While our initial focus was Monterey, Mexico, a Christian leader from Nigeria heard about our work and let us know that the need in his country for ministry to the needy was great. So we started a work there. Since then we have expanded into Haiti, the Dominican Republic, and India. By 2012, we had staff of over one hundred and a budget of over $5 million per year. The expansion has continued. By 2019, the staff had expanded to three hundred, with a budget of $11 million. Eighty-five percent of our staff live abroad as part of our international ministry team.

Five Point Child Development Plan

Since 1997, we have realized the importance of investing on a deeper level in the lives of children. Simply providing for a child's physical needs is not enough. By providing holistic care, rather than merely meeting immediate external needs, we can truly help children to experience complete restoration. With that in mind, the Back2Back 5 Point Child Development Plan was created. It is an approach to orphan care that addresses five crucial areas of child development.

1. *Spiritual:* Alondra is just one of 163 million orphan children in our world, but unlike many orphans, Alondra will wake up tomorrow knowing that she is cared for by her heavenly Father. Through opportunities for spiritual growth such as discipleship and Bible study, we empower children like Alondra not only to discover their tremendous significance as an individual but also to realize their unique purpose in the grand story that God is writing.

2. *Physical:* The dining hall is noisy with voices as Alondra files in with her dorm mates. Back2Back understands the importance of nutrition for children and ensures that the children at our school/orphanage in Monterey will receive healthy meals. Back2Back partners with children's homes to improve quality care for children like Alondra, meeting needs such as mental health and dental

care, nutritious meals, warm clothing, clean water, and shelter. We ensure each child has an opportunity to thrive.

3. *Educational:* Through an emphasis on education, Back2Back invests in the future of children like Alondra so that they might break free from the cycle of poverty. When children have access to education, they are significantly more likely to become self-sustaining individuals who give back to their community. To see that goal realized, we provide each child with tools they need to succeed, tutoring children who are struggling and even offering scholarships to teens who participate in the Back2Back Hope Education Program.

4. *Emotional:* Alondra has two sisters who live in her children's home, but they have little understanding of being a family. Many orphans who grow up in a children's home suffer from psychological issues as a result of past abuse and neglect. By living alongside the children, our staff gain their trust and begin a dialogue of recovery. By offering opportunities for them to seek healing through counseling, we seek to empower the children to work through issues such as anxiety, depression, and attachment disorders. Our goal is that each child would be restored to emotional wholeness.

5. *Social:* The schoolyard is alive with voices as Alondra plays with her best friends, Deynari and Estefi, who are also her roommates. They clap their hands together while chanting a rhyme. Back2Back addresses the need for positive social interaction. We encourage each child to pursue personal growth by offering training and vital skills such as conflict resolution, stewardship, work ethic, independent living skills, and interpersonal communication. By mentoring children in these areas, we empower them to flourish relationally.

Our Focus Areas

In addition to our values, we have four areas of ministry focus: (1) the staff team, (2) child development, (3) in-country national partners, and (4) ministry partners.

1. Staff Team Development

The staff are key players in reaching sustainability for each child. The team strives to meet their spiritual, physical, educational, emotional, and social needs. The team must:

- Be trained and equipped

- Be sustained through financial support

- Have resources for success, such as in-country housing, health benefits, transportation, office space, ministry facilities, etc.

- Be the "right people on the bus"

- Have clear responsibility that defines their role with Back2Back contributing to the sustainability of the orphan child

- Be fully devoted to supporting the infrastructure of the international ministry

- Maintain the culture of Back2Back

2. Child Development

The 5 Point Child Development Plan is Back2Back's filter for what we have to do or not do in each location we serve. It also serves as our tool to measure success toward sustainability with each child we serve. Current child-development programs and future child-development programs secure the success of the child.

3. In-Country National Partners

Our investment in key in-country partners is crucial to the sustainability in the development of the orphan child. It is important that in each country Back2Back serves we invest time and resources into our national ministry directors. They are on the front line. These directors are working daily to meet spiritual, physical, educational, emotional, and social needs of the children they serve. Partnering with national directors in these five areas is part of Back2Back's goal of in-depth development and follow-through. It is of equal importance to invest in the homes and environment of the children and staff. Investing in and working with national partners allows the local Back2Back team to gather and generate local human and economic resources that will work toward the long-term sustainability of the children we serve. Work with churches, organizations, and individuals is another layer of influence in each child's life.

4. Ministry Partners

Back2Back ministry partners are key contributors through programs such as mission trips, child sponsorship, support of Back2Back staff, and general ministry programs. Back2Back's ministry partners invest in the depth and follow-through by contributing both human and financial resources.

Our Core Values for Holistic Orphan Care

God has given us a strong framework for our ministry development.

1. *We value what is best for the child.* The 5 Point Child Development plan provides a filter from which we make decisions. This filter allows us to evaluate the resources and activities provided for the children, ensuring that they serve to meet their spiritual, physical, educational, emotional, and social needs.

2. *We value education and training on trauma-informed care.* We want to communicate God is the hero and He's using us to fulfill His will.

3. *We value healthy Galatians 6 relationships with ministry partners and children.* "Carry each other's' burdens, and in this way you will fulfill the law of Christ" (Galatians 6:2). "For each one should carry their own load" (Galatians 6:5). In Greek, the word for "burden" means something someone is incapable of carrying on their own, while the word for "load" refers to a soldier's backpack, which he was expected to carry. We want to empower ministry partners and the children we serve so they carry their own loads as we come alongside them to help them carry their burdens.

4. *We value education and training of dependency-related issues.* We do not want to be the hero to these kids. We want to communicate that God is the hero.

Conclusion

Back2Back is about the sustainability and development of the orphan child in learning to depend on Jesus Christ as we return them to their community in a way that they learn to be confident and independent. I stand on tiptoe to see what God will do in the lives of these precious children in the years ahead. It has been amazing to see God use the ordinary people of Back2Back, including myself, to do extraordinary work, through His power, for His glory.

14

From Addiction to Wholeness

Rick Kardos

I first met Rick in 2004, when we were both *speaking at an Iron Sharpens Iron conference in New England. He was focused on helping men who were struggling with pornography, and I was speaking on behalf of pureHope, which was addressing all the issues related to biblical sexuality. pureHope had been founded in 1984 as the National Coalition Against Pornography, so both of our ministries were very concerned about the harm of pornography.*

I loved Rick's passion for helping the broken. His personal experience with sexual addiction and brokenness drove him to serve others. He understood the destructive impact that pornography had on men and on their marriages and families. Rick has a knowledge base about the issue that is very special. He had partnered with and received training from Pure Desire, one of the leading ministries in the country on these issues.

We continued to speak at the same conferences and developed a mutual respect that was well beyond a professional relationship. Rick and I discussed the ministry of the Nathan

Project and pureHope. We had the same goal—to see God's people living out wholeness and purity in living for and serving Jesus. In January 2005, Rick decided to become a pureHope staff member, serving as the director of our New England office. We strengthened his ministry with financial resources, with training, and by supplying greater structure, planning, and discipline to his work.

Even after pureHope closed our regional offices, I have continued to be blessed by great times of fellowship with Rick and Vicki. My wife, Sharon, and I have taken two wonderful vacations with them. We always enjoy spending time together, whether it is only a few hours over a meal or for an entire week. As you will see from Rick's story, he is truly an ordinary person who has been blessed by an extraordinary God.

Rick's Story

I was born in Toledo, Ohio, in 1954 and raised in Joliet, Illinois, from second grade until leaving for college. My family was typical for its time. Dad was a World War II veteran, a working man who was home at 5 p.m. each day for family dinner. He and my Mom were happily married for over fifty years. I had two younger sisters, one three and the other five years younger than me. We were pretty much a picture of the ideal American family. Before we moved to Joliet for my dad's work, we attended a Methodist church in Holland, Ohio, a small town just outside Toledo. At that time both my mom and my dad were active in church life, with Dad singing in the choir and me serving as an altar boy.

In Illinois, I enjoyed positive grade school experiences and had pretty good grades and many friends. My sisters and I went to Sunday school at a local Protestant church without our parents, who dropped us off for Sunday school and picked us up after it was over. Sunday school led to confirmation and the invitation to membership at age fourteen. That sounds like a Christian education, but I didn't know Jesus personally at all.

During those grade school years and into junior high, I experienced what is considered in today's study of addiction a significant "father wound." Without any doubt or reservation, I can say my dad loved me and would have done anything to protect and to help me be successful at all times in all ways. But he also wanted to help me, I think, to help him feel better about himself. He began to live vicariously through me. He wanted me to hunt and fish with him, which looked like a normal and enjoyable example of dad and son being together. But he also wanted me to be the best at everything I did, and instead of just enjoying our time together he was constantly pushing me do better. Something felt wrong.

Lest I totally forget Mom in those years, she was the best, from beating me at HORSE and being a better free-throw shooter in basketball to taking me to buy clothes and making it fun. She was a friend and encourager, soft on discipline and the woman who spoiled me at every turn.

One unusual part of my grade school years, at least unusual now when I look back through the lens of an addict, was a preoccupation with girls at all times. I always had a girlfriend, always liking a girl who didn't like me the same way, always chasing someone new, always wanting to be close and hold hands and kiss. To this day I do not know or understand the genesis of these desires, but I do know they led to more of the same as I grew into manhood.

Pornography Addiction

By junior high school, I had walked away from any and all participation in the church. An above-average student, I was invited to and participated in advanced class studies. But that all began to change when I was exposed to written pornography in the eighth grade. That first exposure led me to search for pictures and magazines in my own home. Unfortunately, the search was successful. This swiftly led to an addictive preoccupation with pornography. Today I understand that as the addiction intensified my brain had been "raped" in some ways. It was introduced to feelings and neurochemicals that were part of an escalating process to full-blown addiction to pornography and self-sex.

The addiction led to the desire for physical sexual relationships, which led to compulsive sexual activity with women. Honor-roll grades took a nosedive from lack of attention, study, and priority. My focus began to narrow on the wrong thing. But, and a very big but, my addiction was kept totally secret from all of my family and friends. Shame became an everyday part of my life. My thought, and one I know is common among porn addicts of all ages, was, "I am just more sexual; I need 'it' more." It was a lie that pushed a narcissistic personality that grew like wildfire in those high school years. It was always about me and what I wanted, no matter the pain it caused others. That personality eventually cost me a marriage, a job, and a relationship with my only son.

Those leadership roles in high school student government, friends, and athletics were unimportant compared to my search for more pornography and interaction with girls for my pleasure rather than for any kind of a serious relationship. Today I can look back at that father wound discussed a few paragraphs ago and know that looking for and at pornography and enjoying self-sex was medication. The hurt inside, which I never understood, hurt less, and I felt better. But it was a false better, a short-term better. It only lasted minutes, maybe hours, and it was always followed by a shame I didn't understand. Sooner or later it was always followed by the desire for more.

High school graduation and acceptance into university put me in an environment with zero supervision and much more opportunity to use and then to meet and exploit women. The addiction grew exponentially. This behavior continued during my three years in school in central Illinois, then south Florida and back to Illinois. Missing large parts of class, then missing them altogether and dropping classes, became the norm.

As I look back with a clear understanding of my sexual addiction, I attribute the downhill slide to my struggle with focus, my lack of ability to keep my attention on classwork, and my little follow-though on anything other than compulsive sexual behaviors. My behavior was driven to avoid emotional pain regardless of the feelings of others. Selfishness and narcissism were growing within me.

After college I joined the sales force of a small company in the footwear industry. I began as a regional representative in St. Louis, moved to New England at twenty-four in 1978, and eventually became the national sales manager for a small company in New Hampshire. This personal and financial growth in business looked to others like fulfillment of a young man's American dream. But underneath the public life I let others see was the addiction. That behavior eventually brought my whole world crashing down.

Radical Life Changes

My first wife and I married in 1981. We had one son, who was born in Manchester, New Hampshire. After continuing my secret addiction to pornography, adultery, and emotionally abusive relationships with women outside marriage for eight years, I was introduced to and accepted Christ as my Lord and Savior at age thirty-five. The circumstances surrounding that life-changing event were amazing as I look back. Preparing to board an airplane flying home from St. Louis in fall 1989, I saw a business acquaintance, and we ended up sitting side-by-side on our flight home. During the flight he proceeded to tell me all about his church. After about a half-hour or so I finally asked, "So why all the church talk?" He commenced to tell me about his born-again experience several years earlier at a Billy Graham crusade. That led to a discussion about my life, some of my very serious problems, my desire to improve my marriage, and ending the life of pornography and secret affairs.

Just before we landed, he turned and gave me a tract that asked three questions. "Where did I come from?" "Why am I here?" "Where am I going?" The answers were simple yet profound. "A Creator that loves me more than I could ever imagine." "God sent His Son to the cross for me." "That depends on a decision today." That night on the way home I asked Christ into my life. Always a salesman, I offered Him a deal. Give my life to Him in return for a renewed marriage and an escape from my addiction. Who could imagine it would lead to beginning a ministry of hope and grace for men and their families who struggle with the use of pornography and sexual addiction, but we serve a big God!

Coming to Christ led me to share my secret life of addiction with my wife in 1990. Sharing the secret did not heal our marriage as I had hoped, and we divorced in 1995. It is very important to note our divorce did not have its beginning with a fifty-fifty problem as if she had baggage too. It was about my selfish "all about me" lifestyle and my secrets.

God provided the inner courage to confess my sexual sin, seek out professional help, and begin to make changes in my thinking, not only my behaviors. I slowly began to recover from the addiction and experience a new life in Christ, trying to put the desires and needs of others before mine. But I certainly wasn't delivered, as some in the Christian community call that initial period of sobriety. This was merely the time when sexual relations of any kind and inappropriate emotional relationships with women other than my wife and pornography began to move out of my life.

Attendance at a local Baptist church in 1990 was the beginning of a new Christian life. It was a safe place to listen and learn about God, His son, and His plan for my life. In 1996, I married for the second time, and my walk with Christ received a significant boost. My new wife,

Vicki, was a great example of relying on Christ for strength as a devoted single mom. Her relationship with Him was evident in everything she did. Her working three jobs to provide for her children, hours of dedicated preparation to lead worship at her church, and patience with her children (and me) all demonstrated a vibrant love for Jesus. She uncovered and inspired a desire in me to learn more about Christ. Attending and then joining her strong, Bible-believing church and the experience of meeting her mature Christian friends changed my heart, set my mind on a new path, and created an intense desire to walk with Christ.

Ministry

Early on in our marriage I was invited to be a part of and then help lead and expand the men's ministry at our church. A successful team developed, and we held regular men's events, opening the door for everyone to share their personal stories and begin to minister to each other. Sharing my story of addiction, loss of a marriage, and the broken relationship with my son and renewal in Christ, opened my eyes to the degree of sexual addiction in the church. After sharing my testimony to a group of forty men, eight of them stopped me and asked for help with their struggle with pornography and addiction. I realized that I was not part of a small minority of strugglers.

In 2002, a close brother from the Promise Keepers movement, Brian Doyle (current founder and president of Iron Sharpens Irons conference ministry), invited me to attend a Pure Desire conference led by Dr. Ted Roberts and his team from East Hill Church in Gresham, Oregon.

During the second day of teaching, I felt a powerful and very clear call to minister to men caught up in the struggle with pornography and sexual addiction. That fall, my wife, Vicki, and I visited the Pure Desire headquarters in Oregon and met personally with Ted and his wife, Diane. They taught us how to build our first For Men Only group and eventually For Women Only groups for spouses in New England. These closed, confidential, peer-led groups offered a safe place for men to learn, attain sobriety, and after two to five years of recovery work, to heal.

That fall I experienced a major shift in my picture of God's plan for me. His plan moved me from what He could do to help me grow to how could He use me to help others grow and be healed. Vicki had a similar experience and calling to help women who needed to recover from the harm of their relationships with addicts.

After experiencing success with our first group, Vicki and I co-founded the Nathan Project in 2003. The name is in reference to the role the prophet Nathan played in the life of King David. Our hope was that all men would recognize the need for a Nathan in their lives, a man who would shoot straight with them and tell them like it was when they chose a wayward path. We hoped that when men heard the correcting words of a Nathan, they would own their sin and humbly respond as David did in Psalm 51.

At the start the Nathan Project focused on the local church, speaking with men's leaders and teaching about the dangers of pornography and sexual addiction. As awareness set in and men came forward for help, we began our first For Men Only Group, and Vicki launched the first For Women Only Group. We continued to receive training with Pure Desire and started more groups across New England. Vicki was soon leading For Women Only groups about forty weeks per year in our home in Bedford, New Hampshire.

In 2004, while sharing the dangers of pornography and the issue of addiction versus struggle at a Vision New England—Iron Sharpens Iron conference, I met Rick Schatz, President of the National Coalition for the Protection of Children and Families, ultimately renamed pureHope. It was a national ministry serving the sexually broken and their families and bringing Christian solutions to the problem of sexual addiction in the local church. The mission and vision of pureHope and the vision and purpose of the Nathan Project were strongly aligned, and I joined pureHope's staff as Executive Director for New England in January 2005.

In a few short and exciting years, we expanded through all six New England states. Through the partnership, teaching, and encouragement of Rick Schatz, we began to grow. It is an understatement to say that pureHope provided significant financial support and ministry training. Their support allowed both Vicki and I to prosper in our faith, our ministry, and our personal relationship with each other. Without Rick, his wife, Sharon (now very dear friends as well as partners in ministry), and his entire team, I doubt these words would be meeting this page.

In 2011, pureHope made a strategic decision to close all of its regional offices and eliminated my salaried position of Executive Director. In response to that change, Vicki and I prayed and then, with God's blessing and the support of close friends, restructured the Nathan Project as a standalone ministry under the authority of the elders of our home church. We have continued that relationship and are blessed to have forty active For Men Only groups in New England and a full-time area director in Vermont. It has also been exciting to have one of our best leaders become the Nathan Project area director for the Capitol City region of New Hampshire. He has prospered and now elevated the teaching from For Men Only to a new level and into the New Hampshire state prison as part of his own full-time ministry, Rise Again. We are also developing leadership training forums as well as a new leadership manual. We are working with and launching new group ministries at vibrant churches such as Eastpoint Christian Church in Portland, Maine, Park Street Church in downtown Boston, and two large church-planting groups in the city of Boston and surrounding communities.

Over the past fifteen years, the center of the Nathan Project's growth has been the extraordinary privilege to speak and minister to men at as many as sixty-five Iron Sharpens Iron conferences, six each year, in five New England states. At the largest conference, in Hartford, Connecticut, as many as three thousand men gather to be equipped with the gospel and Christian tools for everyday life. Through these conferences we introduce our work and a Christian solution to the addiction to pornography to as many as seven thousand dads and sons every year. The men hear a vitally important message of hope. In the seminar we offer to equip and encourage them to battle the exposure and quite often the addiction to pornography.

Impact

An exciting testimony to our work happened a few years back. A college student home for Christmas break approached me at his home church, stuck out his hand to shake mine, and said, "Thanks for all you are doing in your ministry. It changed my life." It was an interesting introduction. We had never met, but he explained that a local business owner who had participated in and graduated from a For Men Only group knew his family quite well. When he, as a teenager, fell into the bondage of pornography and addiction, his family turned to this trusted friend for help. He mentored the young man and a few others, and what fruit! That young man is now a pastor, married, and serving in vocational ministry back here in New England!

One of our most exciting engagements, and most challenging, was the invitation to speak at the United States Military Academy—West Point. We were invited by the ministry of the Navigators to present the Nathan Project with an emphasis on specific training to produce For Men Only leaders. The cadets and officers of West Point were looking to build and operate new groups to educate and help men break free not only at the academy but in their future assignments across the world.

In the fall of 2017, the President of Gordon-Conwell and the Dean of Students invited us to a meeting where we discussed the need of the Nathan Project to train new leaders and grow what is now referred to as Men's Healthy Sexuality groups on campus. Through its strong leadership, the seminary is now served by as many as five men's groups, one-on-one counseling, and a new group for wives and female friends of men addicted to pornography. This work is helping men escape the bondage of pornography use that holds them (and, if married, their families and their potential ministries) hostage. When they are free, the ripple effect of this work at Gordon-Conwell will affect the church of Jesus Christ today and for years to come as these men move into full-time pastoral ministry.

My wife, Vicki, has been the director of women's ministries since the Nathan Project's inception in 2003. She has launched and leads For Women Only spousal support and recovery groups. She also trained several leaders now leading new groups in several southern and seacoast communities of New Hampshire. Three years ago, she took an eighteen-month sabbatical from leading the groups to research, write, and publish a new, 210-page workbook/curriculum for use in fourteen-week small groups for wives, ex-wives, and fiancées of men addicted to pornography and other compulsive sexual behaviors. This new workbook is aptly titled *STORM*, an acronym for Surviving Trauma and Overcoming Relational Mistrust.

In addition to *STORM*, Vicki also uses *Changing the Shadow of Our Future*, a ten-week curriculum, written by her and a co-author and focused on breaking free from the co-dependent or abusive relationship a spouse may have with her husband. Vicki, with an excellent team of leaders, has led over forty groups using *STORM* and *Changing the Shadow of Our Future* at our home in New Hampshire.

It's a big problem!

Pornography is the number-one drug of use leading to addiction in the United States. And it is not only unregulated, but it is encouraged! In our sexualized culture, sex sells everything from deodorant to YouTube to internet content for children veiled as toy commercials. In 2018, $33.5 billion dollars were spent on pornography. Every second 28,258 users are watching pornography on the internet. Every day, 2.5 billion emails containing pornographic content are sent or received, and 68 million search queries related to pornography are made. That's 25 percent of total internet searches. *Big* is a dramatic understatement! To make these numbers come to life, consider this—if you began in 1903, the year of the first flight of the Wright brothers, and proceeded to binge-watch all of the pornographic videos that are currently available, you would still be watching those videos in 2018.

We as a society have become desensitized to the tentacles of pornography within our everyday lives. Pornography thrives in the darkness of isolation. It is best dispelled in the light of relationship with others and the love and care that only Jesus Christ can provide.

Scriptures and the love of men who traveled the road from bondage to wholeness before me have transformed the Nathan Project. As mentioned in the story of the name of the ministry, David's words in Psalm 51 undergird all that we teach and all that we share.

In response to these overwhelming statistics and the challenges in our culture, the mandate of the Nathan Project is driven by this scripture:

> The Spirit of the Lord is on me, because he has anointed me to proclaim good news to the poor.

He has sent me to proclaim freedom for the
  prisoners and recovery of sight for the blind,
to set the oppressed free, to proclaim the year
  of the Lord's favor. (Luke 4:18–19)

Another significant scripture that brought us to full-time vocational ministry is from Ezekiel 33. This passage highlights the call and instruction of the watchman.

> Again the word of the Lord came to me, saying,
> "Son of man, speak to your people and say to
> them: 'When I bring the sword against a land,
> and the people of the land choose one of their
> men and make him their watchman, and he
> sees the sword coming against the land and
> blows the trumpet to warn the people, then if
> anyone hears the trumpet but does not heed the
> warning and the sword comes and takes their
> life, their blood will be on their own head. Since
> they heard the sound of the trumpet but did
> not heed the warning, their blood will be on
> their own head. If they had heeded the warn-
> ing, they would have saved themselves.'"
> (Ezek. 33:2–5)

I am blessed and still in awe that our great God would take a broken sinner like me out of bondage to sexual sin and use him for His glory through the Nathan Project. My story is surely one of ordinary people and an extraordinary God.

15

From Abandonment to Embrace

Vicki Kardos

Soon after I met Rick Kardos, I had the *privilege of meeting his wife, Vicki. She complemented Rick's passion and energy with her own skills and abilities. Vicki saw the problem of pornography from the perspective of the woman who had been abused, cheated on, and often abandoned. She saw clearly the failing of the church to address this part of the problem and is determined to bring change.*

Vicki is an amazing writer, teacher, and trainer. She wrote STORM (which stands for Surviving Trauma and Overcoming Relational Mistrust) and more recently has developed an entire workbook for women leaders in For Women Only groups. She has supported Rick through the times of blessings and trials. In many ways she is the emotional and spiritual rock of the Nathan Project.

Rick and Vicki are a great example of two ordinary people who have been brought to wholeness by the grace, love, and mercy of God and who have gone on to do amazing work for our extraordinary God.

Vicki's Story

I was born in Anchorage, Alaska, in 1953. I was a middle child and have an older sister and a younger brother, both serving God today. We are close in age and enjoyed, as siblings, the rewards of growing up in the "Great Land." I would consider us a tight-knit family even though our mother was a strong Christian and our father was not a believer. My father was a generous man, and I deeply loved him, but his alcoholism and unfaithfulness in his relationship with our mother caused pain and sorrow. The difficulties they had may also have contributed to my mother's mental breakdown and the clinical depression she suffered for many years.

Thankfully, God eventually healed my mother in my late teens, and she experienced a return of joy and personal freedom that comes with the will to forgive. She taught me the value of forgiveness and unconditional love. She didn't walk around acting like everything was okay when it wasn't, and I learned that it is okay to not be okay at times. My father was raised in Alaska and tried to instill in us how to deal with hardship in a "buck up" fashion, but I learned in life that moving toward my pain and dealing with it appropriately was healthy. Ignoring it never helped heal the holes in my soul.

I cannot remember a time when I did not believe in God, did not believe He existed, or questioned His love for me. I must have accepted Christ at a young age in Sunday school. Being raised in a Baptist church, I probably asked Jesus into my heart several times just to cement the covenant with Him! Because I do not remember a time I did not know of God, I believe He began working in my heart early in my life. It wasn't until later in my teen years that I resisted, but He never took His hand away.

I was sixteen years old when I made a bold speech to my mom about not wanting to go to church anymore. I had been brought up fairly legalistically, and I guess I thought I had earned the right to sow some wild oats. I am not proud of those years and was not a good influence on some of my friends, but thankfully God cut those years away from Him short. Even when I was tempted to do things I knew were wrong, I can remember God speaking to me. I just didn't want to listen. So much of what I had learned about a relationship with God was somehow tied together in my mind with performance, and that was not the kind of faith I was interested in pursuing.

The Journey Toward Deeper Faith

In the fall of 1973, I went with my sister and my mom to visit my aunt in the Philippines for a few months. At the time, my mother's sister was a Wycliffe missionary translator in Southern Mindanao (currently called the Davao Region) among the indigenous Blaan people. Before I even left Alaska, I sensed that a spiritual change in me needed to happen. There wasn't anything specific on the trip that made the change in my heart except that I know my sister, mom, and the missionaries I had met were praying for me. It was just before Christmas when we returned to the United States. I remember sitting on the bed I was sleeping in and recommitting my life to Jesus Christ. I was nineteen years old, and I have never looked back to a life outside Him.

The Jesus Movement in the early seventies was still in full swing, and Alaska also experienced this revival and a spiritual awakening. In spring 1974, I met a man in a Christian coffeehouse in downtown Anchorage. He was a new believer and had left his cabin in a small Russian fishing village to check out a church in Anchorage. The church's contemporary worship styles were already creating controversy among the evangelical denominations.

Many nonconformist hippies were being saved and exhibited a passion about their newfound faith. This church had opened a new Bible/leadership training school for the growing congregation and community, and was casting a vision to plant churches around the country. In the coffeehouse I overheard this young man with his Jesus-like long brown hair and quiet persona sharing his new faith. I was intrigued and made it my business to hear more about his story. He was interested in attending the new Bible school and moving to Anchorage, where he could meet other Christians and grow in his faith.

It wasn't long before we were both attending Bible school, and we struck up a deep relationship that was beyond friendship. By December 1974 we married with the ambition to be one of the church plants. By fall 1975, we had packed our few belongings in our hippie aqua van with bright flowered curtains and headed down the Alaska Highway (the Alcan) to our first (and last) church plant in California. I was pregnant and expecting our child in early spring 1976.

My husband got a job right away as a roofer, but our excitement was as quick to dry up as the California landscape that year. The drought didn't exactly call for a line of people wanting new roof repairs that year, and we ended up on food stamps and welfare, and having our son delivered by Stanford University medical students. The rather humbling experience didn't last long, but it really taught me the value of money and to take nothing for granted. By fall 1976 our spiritual dream bubble burst, and we returned home to Alaska.

A year later we were delighted to experience the birth of our second child, a girl. It was 1977 and we were able to buy a condo. Things seemed to be on the upswing for us. A couple of years later, we were able to buy a small house, and my husband landed a government job that could provide us with a more secure and comfortable financial future. I wasn't prepared for the dark cloud that would descend on us.

The Breakdown

By 1986 something was wrong, terribly wrong. I was thirty-two years old. It was at this time that I began to journal. Our children were around nine and ten years old. I was scared. I noticed at first small but obvious changes in my husband's spiritual interests, and he questioned our Christian faith, especially mine. He began to spend more time with friends from work after work hours. I could sense his detachment from me, from our family, to something else, and it felt dark and formidable. A fog seemed to invade our home, and my relationship with him felt like it was crumbling. I had dreams that he was going to leave me, and I felt powerless and confused.

I discovered a New Age magazine in his belongings and recognized that this new interest was somehow having a negative impact on us and tearing our family apart. I began to pray against this invisible force. My husband stayed out later at night, sometimes not coming home. One day I got a call from his sister warning me that he was considering divorce. He was done with Christianity, and he wanted no part of the belief system I still embraced. I was shaken to the core. My first thought was, *How will I take care of our children?* I hadn't worked outside the home in years. The enemy of my soul placed a thought in my mind that I would have a breakdown just like my mom.

> For the Spirit God gave us does not make us timid, but gives us power, love and self-discipline. (2 Tim. 1:7)

I can remember sitting down and praying this verse over and over until the fear subsided. I got up and went into the bathroom to wash my face. As I bent down to open a drawer, God spoke to me. "Go call your past orthodontist and ask him to train you as an assistant." It was a clear message, and my heart was pounding in my chest. I thought, *What do I have to lose?* I took a deep breath and, without giving myself time to second-guess the message, dialed the doctor's home phone number.

It was the middle of the week and during usual work hours. The other line rang and was quickly answered by the doctor on the other end. I found myself giving him a brief description of my situation and my need to learn a skill. I told him I would work without pay if they were willing to take me on and train me. It just happened that he had to run home that day for something and was planning a staff meeting the following day. He would talk to the staff and get back to me after their meeting. Two days later he called to say they would hire me and I could start work the following week. This began a thirty-year career for me, from which I just recently retired.

On May 22, 1987, my husband came home in the middle of the day and said he was done with the marriage and was divorcing me. I couldn't believe how calm I felt in that moment. I told him I would not fight him and would release him.

> When you pass through the waters, I will be
>   with you;
> and when you pass through the rivers, they
>   will not sweep over you.
> When you walk through the fire, you will not
>   be burned; the flames will not set you ablaze.
> (Isa. 43:2)

I loved our little house, but I knew we had to sell it. I would need to move home with my parents, who now had a home in Anchorage and a second, winter home in California. My children would have to switch schools. I just did the next thing I needed to do. When the time came close to when I was told I would be receiving divorce papers, my new boss encouraged me to take the children to California to be near my parents. He thought it would be a good support and I would not be alone when the papers arrived. My husband agreed to have them sent to me, but they never arrived. On my birthday I received a letter from him saying he had changed his mind and did not want a divorce.

I will lead the blind by ways they have not
known, along unfamiliar paths I will guide
them;
I will turn the darkness into light before them
and make the rough places smooth.
These are the things I will do; I will not forsake
them. (Isa. 42:16)

This has become my life verse. This is the scripture
God gave me as I prayed about what to do following the
letter. I was still in California and made an appointment
with my mom's pastor to get some counsel. He didn't
know me or my situation, but it was this same verse he
gave me when I was in his office! It was all I needed to
know that God saw me and He heard me. No matter what
my decision was, God would guide me and not forsake
me. I had to return to Alaska to finish training and would
see how sincere my husband was about reconciliation. He
also had received a job transfer to Boston and wanted us
to move with him. The transfer was to take place in a few
months. I returned to Alaska filled with uncertainty, yet
hopeful.

It was September 1987, and something was still persis-
tently bothering me. We had started marriage counseling,
and during a session I brought up my concern over a female friend he had spent time with. Before and during
counseling he continued to say she had only been a friend,
nothing more. I wanted desperately to believe this was the
truth. The day following our counseling session I came
home sick from work.

In the afternoon, I received a call from a woman with
two children whose husband had left her for another

woman. She thought I could provide some encouragement and possibly some legal advice. I was willing to help but mentioned to her that my situation was different in that adultery had not been involved. When our conversation ended, she immediately called my sister to tell her that I did not know about my husband's affair, but someone had seen him and reported to her the details of what she had observed. This was why she had called me. She knew my reality was her reality and was desperately seeking support because I would understand her pain.

The details of what had been witnessed between my husband and another woman (the relationship I had been concerned about) could not be denied. They were too specific and the source too reliable. My sister told me the truth, and my suspicions and that gut feeling of betrayal became my numbing truth.

I went to my pastor and his wife for prayer and waited until I was emotionally stable enough to confront my husband with what had been disclosed to me. When I went to confront him, I was still shaken, yet able to report the facts without losing my composure. God gave me the courage to confront the truth and not be confused by my husband's denial or minimizing. I had not been crazy, nor had I misread the dreams and red flags. I had been lied to. The truth was brought into the light, and because my husband seemed genuinely sorry, I decided the relationship was worth a second chance. This test of faith challenged me even further when he received a job transfer to New England. Though I was cautious, I decided to depend on God for His help, take the risk, and follow him there.

The Move to New England

Flying away from all I had ever known was like getting into an airplane with a parachute and wondering whether it would open when I took my leap with my faith into the unknown. Next to me sat our two young children. The three of us were totally in God's hands, and we would need to trust Him to open the parachute and land us safely into our new life on the East Coast. When the plane was landing, I remember seeing the iconic lit-up clock on the Custom House tower in Boston. In that moment a peace washed over me, and I knew I had made the right decision.

My husband had rented a home in southern New Hampshire. It was early December 1987 when we arrived to our new home. I found a church to attend with our children, and it felt like a safe place to start healing. My husband no longer embraced anything connected to Christianity, but I settled into my new normal the best way I knew how. Sadly, the hope of a new life in the East was interrupted a year later with the onslaught of dreams of infidelity again, and anger rose up inside of me. God also showed me that I was still harboring an unresolved desire to see my husband feel the pain he had reaped on us, and resentment still lingered. This was a breaking point for me to have the Lord reveal my own ugly heart and my need to forgive more fully. Later it became clear as to why this was so necessary at this point. If I did not carve out room in my heart from the past wounds, I would not be able to endure the new ones.

Neither height nor depth, nor anything else in all creation, will be able to separate us from the love of God that is in Christ Jesus our Lord. (Rom. 8:39)

By July 1989 I could see that my husband was unhappy and pulling away again. A job working for a local orthodontist had opened up for me, and I gratefully accepted, sensing that our marriage was at risk again. Around this time, I also met some Christian women who surrounded me with prayer and support. Today they are still some of my closest friends. By September, we were back in marriage counseling, and during the second session my husband declared he was done and wanted a divorce.

The rejection was overwhelming, and for a time the harsh reality of being alone led me down a path of suicidal thinking and self-doubt. I made a decision to stay in New Hampshire for only reasons I can now fully understand. At the time, I thought it would be best to keep the children near their father. A year of separation took me down a pathway of really experiencing the truth of Romans 8:39. I had to learn to love myself again. The month the divorce became final happened in the same month I flew back to Alaska for my father's memorial service. He had passed away from a sudden heart attack. This time I was with the rest of my family when the news of legal closure occurred, and we grieved together both the death of our father and the death of my marriage.

The years passed, and I was busy working jobs, growing in my relationship with Christ, serving as a worship leader in my church, facilitating a Bible study group, and falling more in love with the beauty of my new home state. I rediscovered my talent for painting and love of art. I felt at peace. I had the normal ups and downs of raising two teenagers, and life was challenging financially, but God provided for us in amazing ways beyond what we could have thought or imagined. Out of respect for my family, there is no need for details of some of the challenges we faced, but I will say that by the grace of a mighty God, He brought us through. Today I have a strong, healthy relationship with my children. They are incredibly responsible adults and wonderful parents. They also made it a priority to keep their father in their lives and to love us both unconditionally.

Another Bend in the Road

In 1995, I was introduced by a family to a man who had heard about the single, divorced worship leader in their church. It was the same family whose father had given Rick the Fellowship of Christian Athletes tract (see Rick Kardos' story) that led him into a relationship with Christ. Rick decided to visit my church and meet me. Meeting Rick put me on a rollercoaster ride that has been stormy, exciting, frustrating, confusing, rewarding—many ups and downs. If I were to title the relationship, I would have to steal the title "Amazing Grace." This is the relationship that is bringing to fruition the Isaiah 42:16 verse that God had given me years ago when I was in California awaiting divorce papers. My life with Rick became one of the most difficult paths I have taken on my spiritual journey.

I found Rick to be entertaining and a fun companion. He could carry on a conversation with almost anyone and fill up a room with his presence. With him I realized my desire to share my life with someone again. But there was a side to Rick that annoyed and disturbed me. He could be controlling and manipulative and would push boundaries with me and with other people. He had a hard time with the word "no" and would push to get his way. Rules were for other people, and often he would become too enmeshed in my affairs and the affairs of others without being invited. I resented this behavior and the drama surrounding him. When it seemed more than I could tolerate, his endearing side would show up and win my heart back. It was a whirlwind of emotion and struggle — and it was exhausting.

Rick told me he had (past tense and minimized) struggled with sexual addiction. I had no idea what this meant in reality, nor did I have a clear understanding of the common character traits and tentacles attached to someone with a sex addiction. There were red flags, but I couldn't connect the dots of his behavior to what was beneath the surface of our repetitive arguments and upsets. I could tell Rick really wanted to follow Christ and that he wanted to make changes in his life. His behavior had already cost him his first marriage and caused a sad breach in his relationship with his son. When Rick asked me to marry him, in early 1996, we went to talk to his therapist, who assured me that Rick was ready for a new relationship. My gut was telling me something different, and we both should have listened to it, but we followed through with marriage in June following a very short engagement period. I honestly believe that had I not gone through that time of learning to love myself again after my previous divorce, our marriage may not have survived the torrent of crazy stuff that came with it.

My mother got cancer during the difficult early years of our marriage, and I flew back to Alaska in 1999 to care for her until her passing. Rick was still struggling with sobriety, and because he was angry that I was away from him, he would call me long distance and give me a hard time. I would get off the phone in tears and just could not grasp his lack of empathy for me and what my family was going through. It was mind-boggling. My anger turned to an inner rage.

When I returned to New Hampshire, I signed up for hospice training, thinking that maybe God was leading me to serve in the area of grief recovery. I had been impressed and helped by a hospice group's instruction and service to our family with the care of our dying mother. I volunteered with a local hospital hospice group for two years. I didn't know at the time that the grief training I received would go far beyond working with and listening to families in hospice care and coming to terms with the loss of their loved ones. Grieving losses is also a normal step beyond trauma and betrayal.

The Ministry Begins

Meeting Ted and Diane Roberts of Pure Desire Ministries was a turning point for us. They were already running successful For Men Only and For Women Only support groups in Gresham, Oregon. With their help, we received the resources and information to recognize more clearly the ambiguous nature of sex addiction and how it affects relationships and partners.

It was a relief to discover that what I was seeing and feeling was real and that the rage I experienced with boundary violations was common with other couples caught in the web of sexual betrayal. Though Rick was a good companion, sharing, trust, honesty, and openness, along with being a "team player," were challenging for him. There was so much conflict that I began to feel sick both emotionally and physically. But I also wanted to fight for my marriage and for my health. God firmly planted an authentic love for Rick deep in my heart.

In January 2003, we asked a local church to help us bring the Pure Desire team to New Hampshire for a weekend seminar. It was during this weekend that God began speaking to me about starting a For Women Only support group for wives. I did not want to do this. I was still very angry, and I thought I would just be surrounded by a bunch of other very angry wives. But God wasn't giving up on me. He was relentless in His calling me out to trust Him. By the last day of the seminar, He had me. I would start a group on faith the size of a mustard seed. God would need to be the one to grow my faith. I just needed to obey Him.

In April of that same year, I opened my home to other wives and ex-wives of men dealing with sex/pornography addiction. I still did not feel a sense of calling to this type of ministry but wanted to follow God's leading. In the third week of a fourteen-week support group, the women were sharing their stories—most of them for the first time. The woman sitting to my left was sharing her story when my heart broke for her and for what she was sharing.

You could have heard a pin drop as others in the room only nodded their heads up and down in silence and our tears flowed freely. None of us were alone, and we would begin to heal in the safe environment we could provide for one another. I was never the same after that meeting. That was over sixteen years ago, and whenever a new group is arriving, I am like a little girl looking out the window waiting with excitement for her best friends to arrive. Yes, most of them show up angry, but anger is part of grieving, and God can heal that part just as much as a broken heart. "Ship your grain across the sea; after many days you may receive a return" (Ecclesiastes 11:1).

Today I am the co-founder of the Nathan Project, a ministry for men who struggle with the compulsive use of pornography and sexual addiction and to their families. My position as the executive director of For Women Only groups deals with the wives and ex-wives of these men by providing confidential support groups and resources, including how to set healthy boundaries, guidance through grief and trauma, personal plans in facing financial stress fractures, encouragement, and hope. Since 2003, we have seen hundreds of women pass through these groups and go on to live healthy and productive lives after sexual betrayal in their marriage. Their stories of God's grace offer hope to other women in destructive relationships. We have experienced the unfailing, faithful work of God as we weathered the storm and learned to dance in the rain.

Beyond Betrayal

We recently sold our home and bought a condo in a near-by town. The condo has a magnificent view that looks out over hills off in the distance. The view is a reminder to me of just how great and vast the Father's love is for me and for you. I have been a witness to the fact that nothing is in vain and that God's Kingdom view is far beyond my own scope of brokenness. I have also had the privilege to see God's redeeming power to heal and restore at work in Rick's life. God really can work all things together for good when we allow Him to lead us through the storms of life. Nothing is too hard for Him.

> Behold, I am the LORD, the God of all mankind. Is anything too hard for me? (Jer. 32:27)

> And we know that in all things God works together for the good of those who love him, who have been called according to his purpose. (Rom. 8:28)

Often, when we are in the middle of a dark winter in our lives, it is hard if not at times almost impossible to believe that anything good could come out of what we are experiencing. There were times I clung to this verse in Romans just because God promised it, and if He said it, I desperately wanted to believe Him. I wanted this verse to come to fruition at some point along the way, and I hoped that what I had gone through was worth something bigger and more meaningful than just loss and deep sadness. I can honestly say decades later that God used it all, every tear and trial, to pour eventually into a ministry of healing and a message of God's redemptive love and grace. Many of the women I work with today are just like me. Our stories resonate with one another. We have discovered that none of us is truly alone, even if we felt terribly alone and isolated at times.

This story is not about me, not really. It is about the most significant person in my life, Jesus Christ. I owe even my ability to persevere through the storms of life to Him. The older I get, the more I recognize this truth.

16

From Leadership to
Christian Educator

Gary Sallquist

I first met Gary and Joyce in 1981 when they joined College Hill Presbyterian Church. They were brand-new Christians. Joyce committed her life to Jesus in early 1982, about four months after Gary had. Gary had come out of the business world, so we shared that in common. Both of our lives changed dramatically in 1990 when Gary started his seminary training and I left the business world for full-time vocational ministry. I was asked to be his "elder shepherd" while he was at Princeton Theological Seminary. I really should have been his "younger shepherd"!

While Gary was at Princeton, we walked through all the challenges and troubles that followed him and Joyce. They went through a very trying time in their personal finances, the usual challenges of a rigorous seminary curriculum and the difficulty in seeking ordination within his denomination. This last situation was incredibly painful. Gary and I spent lots of time on the phone and in prayer seeking the Lord's leading about what he

should do. He ultimately decided to pursue ordination with an-
other denomination and I strongly supported his decision.

Gary joined the staff of the National Coalition Against Por-
nography (now pureHope) for a short time while I was serving
as President. This was a wonderful time to spend more time to-
gether and he taught me a great deal about humble service and
leadership. When he began as the headmaster of Miami Valley
Christian Academy in 2001, we continued to share our lives
with each other. Over the past ten years, we have spent more
time together as couples enjoying good food, fellowship, sharing
about families, ministry, and life as fellow believers. This has
been a wonderful time for Sharon and me to grow even closer to
Gary and Joyce. In addition, Gary and I get together for lunch
every four to six weeks, which has deepened our relationship
even more. We truly do love each other as brothers in Jesus.

Gary needed to be part of this book because of our deep
friendship, the impact that he has had on my life, and more im-
portantly to tell his story of the power of God to overcome in-
credible brokenness—the calling of the Almighty out of darkness
to His wonderful light.

Gary's Story

I was born July 7, 1938, in Sioux City, Iowa. My maternal
grandmother was Leona Daggett. She was an on-fire believer, loved singing hymns and went to be with the Lord
at the age of ninety-two. She lived with our family for four
years. She was wonderful to me and wrote a letter to me
daily until I was thirty-five years old. This was a great encouragement and blessing. She found me everywhere I
went! Her faith was strong and deep.

My grandfather, Dr. Frank Daggett, died in an accident at age thirty-four. Death was a frequent visitor in the household, as five of six kids died at early ages. My mom was the only one of the children who survived. She divorced my father when I was four years old and later married Charles. Death continued to afflict my family, as Mom died when she was twenty-nine and I was only nine. I knew Mom dearly loved her family, her parents and me. Because of her experiences with death, she highly valued life and did not take it for granted.

I had virtually no relationship with my father after my parents' divorce. Dad was a veteran of World War II and lost both of his legs in the war. During these years of family upheaval, there was no experience with faith or the church.

My stepmother did not want children, and I felt like an unwelcome intruder. When I was twelve, my dad and stepmom virtually kidnapped me from Cleveland and we moved to Spokane, Washington. From there we moved to a farm in Missouri, where we lived for two years. Then we moved to Omaha, Nebraska. I was fifteen and a sophomore in high school. In contrast to my family chaos, my high school years were a blessing.

University Life and Leadership

I went to the University of Nebraska Omaha, and just like high school, college was a great experience for me. I joined the Pi Kappa Alpha fraternity and had many positive leadership experiences and developed friendships that continued long after graduation. I eventually became the national President of the fraternity. That leadership experience continued to work in me as I also became the President of the Junior Chamber of Commerce in Omaha. The Jaycees were a quality organization committed to developing personal character and contributing to the needs of the community. Their creed speaks to issues of integrity, brotherhood, justice and the value of humanity. Perhaps the most important element of the creed is the first line, which reads, "Faith in God gives meaning and purpose to human life." The entire creed was recited at the beginning of every meeting and this had a great impact on my life.

I married Joyce in June 1960 upon graduation and began work at Northwestern Bell. I worked there for four years before joining Mass Mutual Life Insurance. My years in the insurance industry not only provided for our growing family but were personally fulfilling as well. It gave me the opportunity to meet and serve others.

The Move to Cincinnati and God Changes Everything

After many years in Nebraska, we moved to Cincinnati in spring 1981. Soon after we arrived, I met three very influential people in my life: Jerry Kirk, Bob Marriott, and Gene Ellerbee. Each of these men were deeply committed followers of Jesus and they challenged me about my entire life direction and purpose. Jerry Kirk was pastor of College Hill Presbyterian Church, where Joyce and I started attending soon after arriving in Cincinnati. We were blessed at the church and in November of 1981 I committed my life to Christ. Joyce committed her life to Jesus just three months later, primarily due to the influence of a

Christian education class taught by Ron Rand, the associate pastor at College Hill.

Our son, Steve, graduated from high school and began college life at Clemson in 1983. After graduation from college he married Chrysa. We have been blessed as they have two children, Liam and Emma, who have greatly enriched our lives. They live near us in greater Cincinnati. Both are strong followers of Jesus. Our daughter, Susie, is married to J. P. Rail. They also have two children, John and Rosie, who also bless us.

In the midst of a productive career in the insurance business, I was invited to speak at Hanover College. The night before I was to speak, my bedroom was filled with a bright light and the Lord spoke to me. I was to do three things; wrap up my business, go to seminary, and spend the rest of my life involved in Christian education. I had never before considered any of these three options. The message was so clear that I was faced with the choice of obeying or pretending it didn't happen! Later that morning, I shared this experience with Reverend Simon A. Simon, who was my contact at Hanover. I told him what I had heard from the Lord. His response was surprising, even shocking! He told me that both he and his wife had been praying about when to tell me they sensed that God was calling me to the ministry.

When I returned to Cincinnati, I shared the experience with Jerry Kirk. He told me to share my experience and seek the advice of several friends. I did so, and almost everyone I shared with used the same words in their response. They said, "This is perfect for you." At that point, I was convinced that God was speaking to me, and it was clear that I needed to obey.

Another Amazing Change

I started at Princeton Seminary in 1990 at the age of fifty-two. I was there for three years, and during the time I experienced significant financial trouble. However, I had a wonderful experience at Princeton. I enjoyed the study and working with Dr. Tom Gillespie, the seminary President. He heard in his quiet time that he was to create a position for me so that we could work together. This was a surprise to both of us, as the seminary had never had a position like this before. Working with Dr. Gillespie was a great honor and an important part of my educational experience. This position lasted for nine months, and I got to interact with each of the departments in the seminary. In doing this I learned a great deal about running an educational institution.

Joyce and I experienced a steady succession of miracles during our time at Princeton. One of these was related to our personal finances. We had sold our home, most of our furniture, and one of our cars but were continuing to face a bank loan, which we were in the process of paying off. However, the bank was unjustly calling the loan and we certainly did not have the cash to pay it off immediately. We were facing a crisis and had no way to meet the demands that the bank was putting on us or to pay for the cost of my seminary education. Out of the blue I got a call from Dr. David Crawford, a staff member at Princeton. He informed me that the seminary was awarding a full tuition scholarship for all three years of my training. I had not even heard of this scholarship and certainly had not applied for it. We were unable! But God is always able! This was a miracle of God's grace and care for me and our family.

Full-Time Vocational Ministry Begins

After graduating from Princeton in 1993, it was appropriate to move into the ordination process within my denomination. In contrast to my seminary experience, the ordination process was surprising painful and difficult. I took five ordination exams, covering everything from my knowledge of Scripture to church government and theology. My exams were poorly received and harshly critiqued. On the exam on the Scriptures, "Too biblical" was written across the top! After much prayer, I decided to pursue ordination within a different denomination, the Evangelical Church Alliance, where I was strongly supported and encouraged.

Once I completed the ordination process, I joined the staff of College Hill Presbyterian Church and shortly thereafter the staff of pureHope (then known as the National Collation against Pornography). From 1995–1997 I served with Promise Keepers, a movement empowering and enabling Christian men to serve the Lord and be faithful husbands and fathers. At that time the Promise Keepers ministry was exploding around the country. It was a great ride moved by the Holy Spirit. This ministry started with one conference in 1991. By 1995 there were nine conferences with a budget that had grown to nearly $90 million per year. God's presence at the conferences was a thrilling experience of worship, discipleship, and praise. I was the Director of the National Division of Planned Giving. The Lord blessed my fundraising efforts, and we raised more than $10 million each year through major estate gifts.

The expansive nationwide impact of Promise Keepers was dramatically curtailed at the end of 1997. Four hundred staff were let go, and I was one them. However, God was not letting me go. My next move was to a Christian fundraising organization called Philanthrocorp. This move allowed Joyce and me to remain in Denver and use both my business background and my planned-giving fundraising experience at Promise Keepers. This was a great experience of Christian growth for me.

In 2001 God brought me back to Cincinnati to become the headmaster of Miami Valley Christian Academy. This was a fulfillment of the mission I had received from God back in 1990—that I was to be engaged in Christian education. The school had been started in 1996 and by 2001 included kindergarten through eighth grade. During my time at Miami Valley Christian Academy, the school grew significantly. We added a new grade each year until it covered kindergarten through twelfth grade. We even had to put up a new high school building. This required a significant fundraising effort on my part—and I certainly felt equipped and prepared for this role because of previous ministry experiences.

Even though I officially retired in 2006, I have continued to be actively involved, focusing on three primary activities. The first is to pour my experience and life into Greg Beasely, the present Headmaster of Miami Valley Christian Academy. The second is to serve seventh and eighth grade boys as a mentor and teacher. My mentoring efforts include helping these young men face challenging family needs and even the loss of parents. The painful family experiences from my youth have prepared me to be a companion and trusted friend during these life challenges. The third part of my work for the school has been to lead a major fundraising campaign to dramatically expand the athletic facilities.

I have been blessed to hear the stories of the life-changing experiences of a Miami Valley Christian Academy education from so many graduates. I am thankful to the Lord for allowing me to play even a small role in their lives. God has been so good!

My life as a follower of Jesus has been deeply touched and molded by the Word of God. The Bible has led my ministry and service to my Lord and Savior Jesus Christ. Some key verses have given me great strength, hope, and peace.

> Now faith is confidence in what we hope for and assurance about what we do not see. (Heb. 11:1)

> "For I know the plans I have for you," declares the LORD, "plans to prosper you and not to harm you, plans to give you hope and a future." (Jer. 29:11)

> Do not be anxious about anything, but in every situation, by prayer and petition, with thanksgiving, present your requests to God. And the peace of God, which transcends all understanding, will guard your hearts and your minds in Christ Jesus. (Phil. 4:6-7)

Then you will win favor and a good name in
the sight of God and man.
Trust in the LORD with all your heart and lean
not on your own understanding. (Prov. 3:4-5)

Unless the LORD builds the house, the builders
labor in vain.
Unless the LORD watches over the city, the
guards stand watch in vain. (Ps. 127:1)

My life is living proof that God uses ordinary followers of Jesus to do extraordinary acts of service in His
Kingdom. It is all because of His grace, love, and power
working within His people for His glory.

17

Finding God at Harvard

Rick and Sharon Schatz

I have been reluctant to include a chapter in this book focused on my wife, Sharon, and myself, but a number of friends and colleagues have strongly encouraged me to do so. So here it is!

Rick

I was born in August 1944 in Cincinnati. I have one older sister, Barb, who in the last few years has become a very good long-distance friend. Our family was in many ways typical of others living in the Midwest in the fifties and sixties. We were "good folks," friendly with our neighbors, with a commitment to integrity and hard work. But under that façade we had lots of serious problems in our home. Mom was an alcoholic, and Dad was a traveling salesman who was gone most weeks from Monday through Friday.

Sharon

I was born in September 1945 in Cincinnati and had one sister, Norma, who was twelve years older than me. Because of the large age difference between my sister and me, I was raised essentially as an only child. My dad had only a fifth-grade education, but he was very good with his hands and could fix anything. He had a radiator shop and also repaired cars. When people had trouble with their cars, they brought them to my dad, Vern. No matter how bad the problem was, Dad could fix it! My mom was a bookkeeper and was terrific with numbers. I sure got left out on that skill!

Rick

I went to public schools and was an excellent student. I loved people and was friendly with everyone. I participated in lots of sports—baseball, basketball, gymnastics, and golf. It was golf that I dedicated myself to and by my senior year in high school I was the number-one player on a very good high school team. My interest in golf allowed me to spend time with Dad, as he was at Terrace Park Country Club on the weekends.

There was no expression of faith in our family. We said grace over dinner, but that was it. We rarely went to church except maybe on Christmas and Easter. We had a Bible in our home, but I never even saw it opened, much less read. I knew who Jesus was but never heard about a personal relationship with Him. I was spiritually blind and lost but sure didn't know it.

Sharon

Just like Rick, I attended public schools, studied hard, and got good grades. I first met Rick during grade school, when my family moved to Silverton, a suburb of Cincinnati. I was active in student government and the honor society. Except for one occasion when one of my friends and I got caught playing jacks in the classroom, I was obedient to my parents and teachers.

I regularly attended church with my mom, but Dad did not go. I made a genuine faith commitment to Jesus as my Lord and Savior at the age of nine and was teaching Sunday school to little children by the time I was twelve. My first church experience taught me the holiness of God, and I learned to fear Him. He had saved me, but the idea of Him loving and caring for me was somewhat overshadowed by my fear of Him.

Rick

When I was a junior in high school, I began to date Sharon (the best thing I ever did other than finally making a commitment to Jesus). She was genuine, kind, and overall a great person. I was taken from the first date! We dated all through the rest of high school and then through our college days at the University of Cincinnati. Those years were filled with great times together and lots of fun at the Delta Tau Delta fraternity parties. We were married the day after graduation from the University of Cincinnati, on June 16, 1967.

Sharon

I was one year behind Rick in school, but we graduated at the same time because I was in a four-year speech and hearing therapy program and he was in a five-year chemical engineering program. These were wonderful times in many ways, but my life was dramatically changed when my mom committed suicide during my sophomore year in college. I had been planning on transferring to Ohio State University after my sophomore in college, but the death of Mom changed all that. I decided that it was best for me to stay home with Dad. That allowed Rick and me to continue dating and building our relationship, which led to our marriage. While the loss of my mom left a huge hole in my heart, I am thankful to God that He brought this about in my life.

Rick

After graduating from the University of Cincinnati, Sharon and I left Cincinnati and moved to Boston, where I attended the Harvard Business School. My children still think the school made a mistake in letting me in! The first year at the business school was incredibly challenging. The time demands were really overwhelming. We did not go to church for the first fifteen months of our marriage. That was typical for me but a great disappointment to Sharon. As my second year at Harvard started, Sharon suggested that we begin going to church. Translated from the Greek she really meant, "Rick, you need to come to know my Jesus." I was open to the idea, and we began attending the Newton Presbyterian Church, which was within walking distance of where we were living. God had orchestrated where we were living in miraculous ways, but space prevents me from telling the full story of that.

Newton Presbyterian was the first really good experience I had ever had in church. The pastor was Burt Smith, and he reminded me of my father. He was handsome, outgoing, and talked about a personal relationship with Jesus. This was brand new for me. Then an amazing thing happened. The church was going to hold a renewal weekend in November, and a group of people from Cincinnati were going to come and share what life in Jesus was all about. Jerry Kirk was the pastor and leader of this team. He preached on Friday night, Saturday night, and Sunday morning. On Sunday night, he challenged everyone to make a personal commitment to Jesus. I went forward and gave my life to Christ. This changed everything.

Sharon

Newton Presbyterian was a brand-new experience for me. I learned about the love of God and that He cared personally for me and had a wonderful plan for my life. My heart was very full. You can imagine how thrilled I was when Rick made his commitment to Jesus. We joined a small fellowship group, and when graduation from Harvard came along in May 1969, it was very difficult to leave. But the good news was that God had called us back to Cincinnati as the place for Rick to start his career and for us to start our family.

Rick

Back home in Cincinnati I was starting three simultaneous life journeys—a career in business, a family, and faith. I had great career learning experiences in the two companies I worked for. I was Vice President for International Marketing and Planning for Xomox Corporation, where I worked for fourteen years. This work took me all over the world. The way I put it, traveling to Europe seems great to everyone who has never done it. Airplanes and hotels get old in a big hurry. In 1984, I resigned from Xomox and started my own business in the recreational waterpark industry. With Surf Cincinnati I was done with travel and got to stay home with Sharon and our growing family.

The Lord gave us three wonderful sons during this time—Mark was born in 1970, Brett in 1972, and Tim in 1978. Each one is gifted in many ways. All three were excellent students and very good soccer players. Sharon and I talk about the fact that we saw over two thousand soccer games with our boys. That is not much of an exaggeration! Each one of our sons made a commitment to Jesus at an early age. They were each deeply involved in church and grew in their faith during their high school years.

My faith journey was centered on College Hill Presbyterian Church and a number of other ministries. I served on the boards of On Target prison ministry and the Spiritual Counterfeits Project, a cult research group in Berkeley, California. At College Hill I served on the elder board and was active in teaching adults through the Christian Lay Academy. R. C. Sproul was on the staff of College Hill from 1968–1971 and was very influential in my growing knowledge of the Bible and the love of theology. In 1978, he asked me to be part of the International Council on Biblical Inerrancy. This was life changing, as I got to learn from men such as J. I. Packer, Jim Boice, R. C. Sproul, Roger Nicole and other world-renowned theologians.

Sharon

Our early years back home gave me the opportunity to focus my time and energy on our sons. God had given them to Rick and me and we were committed to "raise them up in the nurture and admonition of the Lord." While Rick was working hard and traveling, I got to be a stay-at-home mom. This was an enormous privilege and blessing. I poured my life and faith into Mark, Brett, and Tim.

I was very active at College Hill, serving in the Sunday school for children. To put it mildly, I love children! God has called me to serve the little ones He sends to me, and it is a great joy to do so. I also participated in Bible studies and fellowship groups, so as I was pouring my life into our children and the children of other families, God was busy growing me to be more like Jesus. I have always loved God's Word and had time to read and study the Bible on my own as well as with others.

Rick

In 1990, Jerry Kirk, my former pastor at College Hill, came to me and asked whether I would leave the business world and enter into full-time vocational ministry. He wanted me to join him at the National Coalition Against Pornography. I had considered this change before, and after prayer and getting Sharon's counsel, I said yes. This was the beginning of a faith journey with Jerry and others that has now lasted for nearly three decades. I am sure that most of my Harvard Business School classmates thought I lost my mind, but I have never looked back on the decision. Serving with the National Coalition Against Pornography, which is now pureHope, has brought great blessings, joy and fulfillment to my life. I have had the opportunity to speak and preach throughout the United States to parents, pastors, and church leaders. This work has also allowed me to speak in Canada, Mexico, Ireland, and Namibia. I have had the privilege of working with giants of the faith such as Paul and Kay Rader, the former worldwide leaders of the Salvation Army; Cardinal Bernadin of the Roman Catholic Church; and Tom Trask, the retired General Director of the Assemblies of God. How good can it get!

I left pureHope in 2014 and joined Jerry at the Prayer Covenant. This has been another amazing adventure. In just four years we have discipled over 2.6 million children in a lifestyle of prayer, and over 150,000 have made a first-time commitment to Christ. The testimonies of changed lives and worldwide ministry through the Prayer Covenant are clearly the work of God as the Holy Spirit is moving in power, love, and grace.

I was a founding elder of Evangelical Community Church in 1995. It has been wonderful to serve Evangelical Community Church on the elder board, as part of the teaching team for our adult Sunday school and as chairman of the Missions Committee. A special blessing has been to be the accountability partner for my pastor, Rich Lanning, for the past three years.

Sharon

God has continued His calling on my life to children as He has given me the privilege and honor of teaching our three- and four-year-olds about the love of God, the great truths of the gospel and the reliability and power of the Bible. My goal is to demonstrate the love of Jesus for them—not just talk about it but to be Jesus with skin on for them. These little ones really do learn, and they "get it." I am blessed by them and pray that they are blessed by me.

I have been participating in women's Bible studies at church. Teachers such as Nancy Guthrie and Beth Moore have blessed me immensely. To more fully understand God's Word and what it means to live as a faithful follower of Jesus is an exciting, challenging lifelong journey. My life has also been enriched through two women's fellowship groups that I meet with regularly. To learn and live the "depth and riches of God" brings me great peace and joy.

My ministry to children has expanded beyond Evangelical Community Church as I have been volunteering to lead reading groups of first graders at Mars Hill Christian Academy for the past four years. Mars Hill is a classical Christian education school where two of our grandchildren attend. What a blessing to see these children grow in their ability to read and their love in doing it.

Rick and I have taken a number of adult classes at Mars Hill. The professors are amazing, and we have both been challenged to understand more of God's Word through these studies which have included the life of David, Christian ethics, the parables, and apologetics.

Rick

My spiritual walk has been changed over the years by a growing and disciplined prayer life. One key to this has been my practice of writing my prayers down, which I have done for more than thirty years. I learned this from Bill Hybels, pastor for many years at Willow Creek Church in Chicago. Another vitally important element of my growth in prayer was a teaching by Dick Eastman, President of Every Home for Christ. He taught me the value of having a structure for my prayer time. These two practices have changed and blessed me. However, I believe that I have only graduated from kindergarten as a man of prayer. Thankfully I am still learning.

Another point of growth for me has been the practice of reading through the Bible in a disciplined way. I have done this with other brothers and sisters, including my wonderful bride, Sharon. I have developed my own reading program for thirteen weeks, twenty-six weeks, and fifty-two weeks. The pace that works best for me is the twenty-six-week program.

I would be remiss in not mentioning the opportunity to send weekly texts to my three oldest grandchildren and now five other family members and friends. The texts begin with "How is school?" and "How is soccer?". But the real thrust of this is to share the Rick Schatz commentary on a book of the Bible. Over the past four years, I have been through the Psalms, Galatians, the Gospel of John, and a significant portion of Deuteronomy. I have just started through 1 Peter with some of them. My hope and prayer in doing this is to bless, encourage, and disciple members of the next generation.

We Serve a Miracle-Working God

Rick

God has called and blessed our lives in amazing ways over the years. We have had the privilege of serving Him in various ways. We are examples of ordinary people, extraordinary God. God has been faithful to us through both the blessings and challenges of our lives. There are many examples of God's miraculous work on our behalf. We will only highlight three of them.

First is the way that God directed us to live in the attic of a particular home in Newton, Massachusetts, when I attended Harvard. We found that there was no married student housing available for us and were very discouraged by the places that we explored. Then God opened the door for us through a two-week-old newspaper that we found. God does have a sense of humor! The home at 27 Marlboro Place turned out to absolutely perfect. The location was great for Sharon to work in the Waltham school district as a speech and hearing specialist and for me to get to school. But by far the most important part of this location was that it was within walking distance of the Newton Presbyterian Church, where I eventually made my personal commitment to Jesus.

Second is the way that God had given both of us very good health for many years until I was diagnosed with a very rare form of cancer called amyloidosis in 2012. We had to travel to Boston to find a doctor who had expertise in the diagnosis and treatment of the disease. Our son, Tim, played a critical role in doing the research, and Sharon found Dr. Raymond Comenzo at the Tufts Medical

Center, who would see us immediately. Dr. Comenzo was and is just amazing and continues to be much more than a doctor to us.

The prognosis for me was not very good. The disease is fatal in many cases. I was blessed in that the greatest impact was in my kidneys, not my heart or brain. I have been through two six-month chemotherapy sessions and a stem cell transplant over five years ago. For most of the past seven-plus years, I have been able to work, exercise, and serve our great God with energy and His strength. We don't know what the future of this disease will be, but we know that God has us in the palm of His hands.

Sharon

The last miracle is what I have called our "adventure." We were returning from our annual Hilton Head family vacation in July 2016 when Rick had a medical emergency. He passed out while driving on Interstate 75 North near Jellico, Tennessee. The car rolled eight or nine times but did not careen down a very steep embankment. I wound up with fifteen broken ribs, a broken nose, and a broken clavicle. Rick had eleven broken ribs, a compound fracture of his left arm, and a severe cut on the top of his head. But we survived the crash! It had been raining, and the rain stopped in time for us to be transported by helicopter to the University of Tennessee Knoxville, which it turns out is the finest trauma hospital in all of Tennessee. We were expected to spend about three weeks in the hospital there but were released after just nine days. Our son, Mark, was able to stay at the hospital with us and was our advocate with doctors, nurses, the rest of our family and great friends who came from Cincinnati to help us. He was able to get important things done when we were absolutely unable to do so.

Within a few minutes after the adventure began our daughter-in-love Sarah, Tim's wife, contacted churches and friends in Cincinnati, who started a massive outpouring of prayer on our behalf. Through our connections with pureHope and the Religious Alliance against Pornography, this prayer chain reached around the world and God heard and answered those prayers. We were transported to Cincinnati by our son, Brett, and by Tim and Karen Jones, some of our most incredible friends. They drove from Cincinnati to pick us up and then took us back home. We then spent nine days of rehab at the Drake Center and then went to our home in Mason, Ohio. We did need a few months of outpatient care but have come through the adventure essentially without any significant problems. Our God is great, good, and amazing. He is a miracle-working God, and we are thankful for all the ways He has done so in our lives.

Recent Development

Rick

By August of 2019, I had been in remission for nearly five years from the amyloidosis cancer that originally hit me in 2012. I was feeling great without any indications of any sickness, but the doctors found that the disease had come back. I immediately started a new treatment regimen and have again gone into remission. Praise the Lord! At the time of writing this, I am undergoing one chemotherapy treatment each month. This is my fourth time through treatment, and Sharon and I certainly hope that we will continue to be blessed with God's healing work. But no matter the outcome, we are in a wonderful place—God's loving arms. We are at peace and have placed our hope in Him. Your prayers would be greatly appreciated.

Closing Thoughts

The past year has been a great joy. I have been able to spend hours interviewing friends and fellow servants of Jesus. My prayer is that their stories will encourage, inspire, and challenge you. None of these individuals is perfect, but they are all pressing on to the upward call in Jesus. Many have come from great family and individual brokenness, but they have each answered the call of God to serve our King. Their lives demonstrate the truth that there really are no ordinary Christians. What God needs is not our skills, brilliance, or capabilities but only our availability. Answer the call. You will be blessed in the journey!

Acknowledgments

I have had the idea for this book for about two years, but it would never have become a reality without the partnership of Stephen Eyre. He and I have spent many joyful and challenging hours writing and rewriting the stories of these saints. Stephen has brought his wonderful skills and energy to *Ordinary People Extraordinary God*. Thank you, my dear brother and friend.

My hope and prayer is that the final acknowledgment for any good this book might prove to be would go to the living God, Father, Son, and Holy Spirit. I do pray that God will use it in some small way to inspire His people and bring Him glory, honor, and praise.